Mary Rose

Mary Rose

Tudor princess,
Queen of France,
the extraordinary life of
Henry VIII's sister

DAVID
LOADES

AMBERLEY

First published 2012

Amberley Publishing
The Hill, Stroud
Gloucestershire, GL5 4EP

www.amberley-books.com

Copyright © David Loades, 2012

The right of David Loades to be identified as
the Author of this work has been asserted in
accordance with the Copyrights, Designs and
Patents Act 1988.

ISBN 978 1 4456 0622 4

British Library Cataloguing in Publication Data.
A catalogue record for this book is available
from the British Library.

Typeset in 10pt on 12pt Sabon.
Typesetting and Origination by FonthillMedia.
Printed in the UK.

CONTENTS

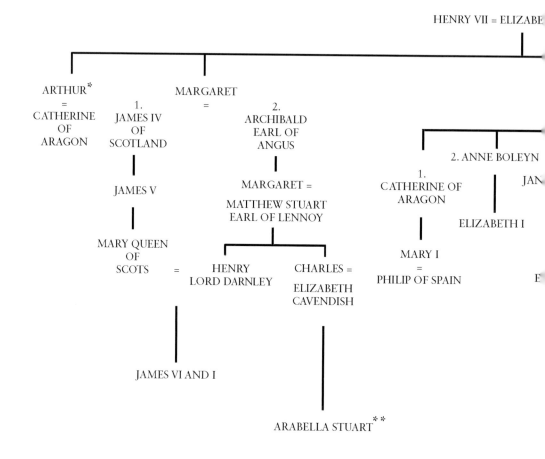

HENRY VII = ELIZABE[TH]

ARTHUR*
=
CATHERINE
OF
ARAGON

MARGARET
=

1.
JAMES IV
OF
SCOTLAND

2.
ARCHIBALD
EARL OF
ANGUS

2. ANNE BOLEYN

1.
CATHERINE OF
ARAGON

JAN[E]

JAMES V

MARGARET =

MATTHEW STUART
EARL OF LENNOY

ELIZABETH I

MARY QUEEN
OF
SCOTS

=

HENRY
LORD DARNLEY

CHARLES =

ELIZABETH
CAVENDISH

MARY I
=
PHILIP OF SPAIN

E[

JAMES VI AND I

ARABELLA STUART**

*   DIED 1502
**   CLAIMANT TO THE THRONE, 1603
+   JANE WAS QUEEN FOR 9 DAYS IN 1553
++   CATHERINE WAS THE PROTESTANT CLAIMANT AS HEIR IN THE 1560s
+++   DIED UNMARRIED IN 1552

1. Genealogical Table

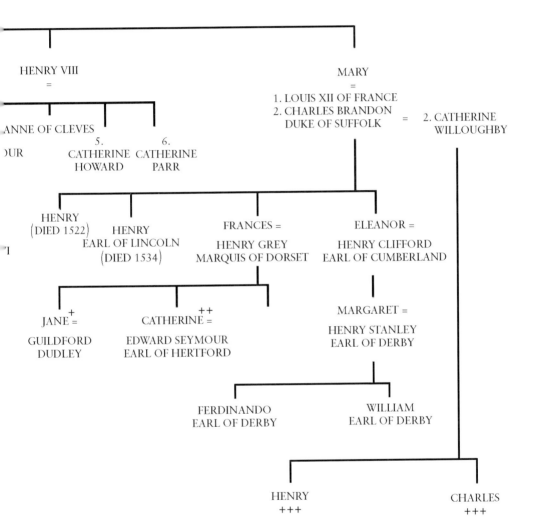

ORK

HENRY VIII
=
ANNE OF CLEVES
OUR

5.
CATHERINE
HOWARD

6.
CATHERINE
PARR

MARY
=
1. LOUIS XII OF FRANCE
2. CHARLES BRANDON
DUKE OF SUFFOLK

= 2. CATHERINE
WILLOUGHBY

I

HENRY
(DIED 1522)

HENRY
EARL OF LINCOLN
(DIED 1534)

FRANCES =
HENRY GREY
MARQUIS OF DORSET

ELEANOR =
HENRY CLIFFORD
EARL OF CUMBERLAND

JANE +
=
GUILDFORD
DUDLEY

CATHERINE ++
=
EDWARD SEYMOUR
EARL OF HERTFORD

MARGARET =
HENRY STANLEY
EARL OF DERBY

FERDINANDO
EARL OF DERBY

WILLIAM
EARL OF DERBY

HENRY
+++

CHARLES
+++

PREFACE

Royal princesses are always interesting, and those who lived in the days of strong personal monarchy especially so. Mary Tudor was Henry VIII's younger, and favourite, sister; the fifth child and third daughter of Henry VII and Elizabeth of York. Little is known of her childhood and upbringing, except that it was heavily influenced by her paternal grandmother, Margaret, Countess of Derby. Her father seems to have shown little interest in her, except to deploy her, along with her sister Margaret, on the international marriage market, but that was the common experience of kings' daughters. At the age of thirteen she was betrothed to the eight-year-old Charles of Ghent, and seems to have enjoyed the prospect of being Princess of Castile. She grew up to be beautiful, intelligent and emotional, but not at all intellectual, and her usefulness to her brother was abruptly terminated early in 1515 by her impulsive marriage to Charles Brandon, Duke of Suffolk, Henry's closest friend. This was a direct result of having been wedded against her will to the elderly Louis XII of France by the terms of the Anglo-French treaty of 1514, and was the subject of fascinated speculation at the time – and since. Thereafter she continued to be known as 'The French Queen' as well as by her proper title as Duchess of Suffolk, but her political role was at an end, so she became an ornament around the court, and a great lady on the Duke's estates.

Her life has attracted a certain amount of attention, including a French biography published in 1749, and a more studious attempt by Mary Croom Brown in 1911; however, most of the interest has been fictional, or popular like Maria Perry's recent *Sisters of the King*. The best scholarly study published within the last half century is W. C. Richardson's *Mary Tudor: The White Queen*, which appeared in 1970. A lot of research has appeared since 1970, including a study of her letters published in 2011, and this, although directed only partly at Mary, is nevertheless relevant to her context, so a further biography is therefore justified. She lived in interesting times, and her support for Catherine of Aragon, Henry's first wife, cast a shadow over relations with her brother in the last years of her life. He nevertheless remained fond of her, and of her rather dim-witted husband, and continued to include them in his social round. For that reason alone she is worth another study, because very few crossed Henry and retained his regard. It was a unique achievement which has been too little thought about.

A lifetime of working on the Tudors, and recently an investigation into Mary's arch-enemies the Boleyns, lie behind this work, and obligations too numerous to list have been incurred. However, mention should be made of the Oxford University History Faculty, which has given me a base, and access both to graduate seminars and to the Bodleian Library, for all of which I am profoundly grateful. I am also grateful to

Jonathan Reeve of Amberley Publishing, who accepted it as a worthy project, and to my wife Judith, who provides unfailing support.

David Loades

INTRODUCTION:
HISTORIOGRAPHY &
BACKGROUND

Mary has always been of more interest to the purveyors of fiction than to historians. This was as true of the author of the *Suffolk Garland* as it was of Jean de Prechac in the seventeenth century, Marguerite de Lussan in the eighteenth, or Russell Garnier in the twentieth. Her story was always good for romantic reconstructions, and the real woman has been largely lost sight of among these stories and legends. Typically Mabel Cleland, writing in *The American Girl* in the winter of 1932/33, called her piece 'The Laughing Princess', a name which Mary would scarcely have applied to herself.[1] In fact the historiography of the French Queen is a thing of shreds and patches, with a heavy concentration on the circumstances of her two marriages, to Louis XII of France in November 1514, and to Charles Brandon, Duke of Suffolk, in March 1515. Before that she was betrothed to Charles of Ghent, the future Emperor Charles V, and she consequently plays an important, though largely passive, role in the diplomatic history of the period 1508–15. It is in such a guise that she appears in all the standard histories of the period, most notably in J. J. Scarisbrick's biography of Henry VIII (1968), where

13

an attempt is made to assess her importance. She also features largely in S. J. Gunn's study of Charles Brandon (1988), which not only examines the details of her two marriages using some new material, but also considers her role as Duchess of Suffolk, both at court and on his extensive estates.² Her support for Catherine of Aragon he considers to have been very influential in determining the Duke's political role between 1529 and 1533. She is considered briefly in Mary Anne Green's *Lives of the Princesses of England* (1855), and rather more fully in Agnes Strickland's *Lives of the Tudor Princesses* (1868), both of them based largely on Hall's *Chronicle*.³

The first modern biography, making extensive use of the calendars of state papers, published in the late nineteenth century, is that by Mary Croom Brown, which appeared in 1911. This quotes lavishly from the Venetian despatches, and contains complete accounts of all the ceremonies in which Mary was involved. It is full and accurate in its descriptions of the costumes and jewellery which were deployed, and on the pageants which accompanied her entry into Paris after her wedding in November 1514. The woman encased in all this ritual appears from time to time, but Brown regarded her as a largely ornamental creature, asserting herself only occasionally. Her determination over her union with Brandon is treated as being largely emotional in its inspiration, and an attempt to escape the attentions of Francis I.⁴ Much more satisfactory to the critical historian is the study by W. C. Richardson, *Mary Tudor: The White Queen* (1970), which makes a serious attempt to assess the importance of the King's sister in the politics of the period. This means a heavy concentration on the period before 1520, and considerable reliance on contextual analysis. The first-hand personal evidence relating to Mary herself being notably scanty, Richardson makes extensive use of contemporary views on the role of women, and on their education and training, applying these to his subject in general terms. His discussion of her character and career is one of the best so far produced, but a lot of research has been conducted since 1970, most notably by Stephen Gunn (1988) and by Michael Jones and Malcolm Underwood in their study of Lady Margaret Beaufort (1992).[5] Very recently has also appeared a new and original study, based largely on Mary's surviving letters, *The French Queen's Letters: Mary Tudor Brandon and the Politics of Marriage in Sixteenth-Century Europe*, by Erin Sadlack. In so far as this is a biography rather than a literary study, it argues that Mary was a shrewd and manipulative operator, well versed in the political functions and limitations of her position. While not questioning the importance of her emotional reactions, Dr Sadlack presents a well-read and thoughtful young woman, who took risks and assessed the consequences. It was not her fault that her French revenues were cut off by the war of 1522–25, and her attempts to recover her income thereafter were sensible and pragmatic. However, the emphasis is very much on the written word, and on the influence of the courtly cult of chivalry rather than upon the historical context of her life.[6] So the time has probably come for another look at Mary Tudor, and at her relations with the men in her life – not only her husbands but also her brother. Unavoidably Henry VIII features largely in the investigation which follows.

In April 1483 Henry of Richmond was in exile at the court of Francis II, Duke of Brittany. He had been there since 1471, when, as a fourteen-year-old escorted by his uncle Jasper, he had fled from the advancing armies of King Edward IV. He had been born in 1457, and was the only son of Edmund Tudor, Earl of Richmond, and of Margaret Beaufort, the daughter of John, Duke of Somerset, who had died in 1444. John having been a grandson of John of Gaunt, the third son of King Edward III, Henry had a remote claim to the Crown of England.[7] He was in fact the last male heir of the Lancastrian line, and Edward IV made periodic attempts to have him extradited, using all sorts of blandishments without success. In exile he had gathered round him a small 'court' of Lancastrian diehards, but as Edward had two healthy young sons to succeed him, Henry's prospects of ever ascending the throne seemed remote. This also was the view of his mother, married since 1472 to her fourth husband, Thomas Lord Stanley, who was doing her best to protect his interests in England. Margaret's marriage had given her a link to the powerful Woodville clan, and consequently a place within the Yorkist establishment. These contacts she used in an attempt to reconcile her son with the King, and in the summer of 1482 she seemed to have succeeded. In an agreement which was drawn up in the King's presence on 3 June, the estates of Margaret's mother, the Duchess of Somerset (who had died in May), were so disposed as to give Henry an inheritance worth 600 marks a year, provided that he returned from exile and submitted to the King's grace.[8] More was expected, and a marriage between Henry and Elizabeth, Edward's eldest daughter, was discussed. They were within the prohibited degrees of affinity and that would require a dispensation, but such things could be arranged. The King also appears to have been considering restoring the exile to his earldom of Richmond. However, all this was conditional upon Henry returning to England, and that he was reluctant to do, in spite of his mother's assurances. Although Edward now appeared to be conciliatory, there was too long a history of mutual suspicion and distrust to be overcome quickly.[9]

Then on 9 April 1483 Edward IV died. At first this did not seem likely to make much difference, because his young son was proclaimed as Edward V, and preparations for his coronation were pressed ahead. However, on 6 July the young king's uncle, Richard of Gloucester, who had been Lord Protector, was crowned instead as King Richard III on the pretext that Edward V was illegitimate.[10] Edward and his brother Richard disappeared into the Tower of London, and the Queen Dowager took sanctuary at Westminster. Richard's coup had been ruthless and not without bloodshed, but Margaret's first reaction seems to have been to accept it, and she played a prominent part in the coronation celebrations. She seems at first to have been disposed to seek a deal with Richard similar to that which she had made with Edward IV. However, Lord Stanley's Woodville connections made him suspect to the new king, and Queen Elizabeth herself remained in sanctuary, so Margaret took a calculated and highly dangerous risk. Abandoning Richard, she threw in her lot with those conspirators who were fomenting rebellion against him. Negotiations for a Tudor–Plantagenet wedding were resumed with Elizabeth, using Margaret's physician Lewis Caerleon as an intermediary, while communications were maintained with Henry in Brittany. Several of Margaret's servants were involved in the Duke of Buckingham's rebellion in the autumn of 1483, and Buckingham wrote to Henry in September, inviting his participation in the revolt. He started by claiming to act in the name of Edward V, but apparently convinced that Edward was dead, then switched his allegiance of Henry of Richmond, a move undoubtedly motivated by the latter's mother.[11] When the rebellion collapsed and Buckingham was executed, Lady Stanley therefore stood in considerable danger, and although she escaped attainder in the parliament of 1484, her estates were confiscated. With them went Henry's inheritance, and any prospect of reconciliation with Richard's government. However, there were compensations. In the first place, the Yorkist party had been split down the middle by Richard's actions, and several prominent members of the Woodville affinity, including the Marquis of Dorset, joined Henry in Brittany, implicitly recognising his title to the throne. Secondly, in the cathedral at Rennes on Christmas Day 1483, Henry solemnly swore to marry the younger Elizabeth, when he had regained his kingdom. This was the result of a renewed agreement between the two dowagers, and was to be of the highest significance for the future.[12] Richard recognised the threat, and renewed his brother's attempts to secure Henry's person. Taking advantage of the illness of Duke Francis II, he almost succeeded, and drove the fugitives over the border into France, where the Regency Council of Charles VIII considered his appeal for support. More positively, Richard patched up his relations with Elizabeth, and persuaded her to withdraw her consent to her daughter's marriage, a success which his own fate in 1485 rendered nugatory.

At the beginning of 1484, Richard was riding high. The parliament which met on 23 January dutifully attainted not only Henry and his uncle Jasper, but also those numerous Yorkists who had joined his cause, including the bishops of Ely, Salisbury and Exeter.[13] Margaret's estates were transferred to her husband, Lord Stanley, for life, in what was probably a conciliatory gesture. Before the parliament was over, the King secured the oaths of all the Lords spiritual and temporal for the recognition of his son, Prince Edward, as his heir, and came to terms with the Queen Dowager, as we have seen. He must have seemed secure. However in early April his son died, leaving him in a dynastic wilderness, and Henry of Richmond began to assume a more serious role in his calculations. Duke Francis was a sick man, and with only his daughter Anne as his heir, a French takeover of Brittany seemed likely. This the Duke's council was determined to prevent, and Richard seized the opportunity to offer military support in return for the surrender of his attainted fugitive. A deal was done on 8 June, but Henry got wind of the plot and, by a subterfuge which involved disguising himself as a servant, managed to slip over the border into Anjou.[14] When the Duke discovered what had happened, his indignation was reserved mainly for his own council, which had sold Henry so unworthily, and he generously allowed the rest of the English exiles to join Henry in France. They were afforded an honourable welcome, but the Regency Council put the question of supporting any bid against Richard on hold for the time being. The minority government was not attracted by the idea of war with England.[15] Nevertheless, in the latter part of 1484 Henry's stock began to rise. He was joined by the Earl of Oxford, a Lancastrian stalwart who had been imprisoned in the castle of Hammes, near Calais, but who now broke out and brought most of the garrison with him. This was seen as an indication of increasing support, and the Council began to take his royal pretensions seriously. Then on 16 March 1485 Richard suffered another blow with the death of his queen, Ann. Whereas the death of his son had been seen by his enemies as a divine judgement, the death of the Queen was laid at Richard's own door, because it was thought that he had poisoned her in order to marry his niece, Elizabeth, a rumour fuelled by her mother's improved relations with the King. There was much talk of this marriage, but no serious evidence that it was ever entertained.[16] What did happen was that Richard felt compelled to issue a formal denial that he had been responsible for his wife's death. As Henry's credit was rising in France, so Richard's was declining in England, and at about the time of Ann's death, the Regency Council, headed by the King's sister Anne of Beaujeu, decided to back the former's bid for the Crown of England.

Henry, meanwhile, had begun to assume the name and style of King, and further recruits joined him, notably Richard Fox, who had been studying in Paris. Communications with his supporters in England, which had continued intermittently throughout his period of exile, now began to assume a more purposeful air. Messengers went surreptitiously to and fro, with his mother, with Lord Stanley, with John Morgan with Walter Herbert and several others, soliciting their support. In return word came out of Wales that Rhys ap Thomas and Sir John Savage were wholly committed to him, and that Reginald Bray was collecting funds on his behalf. Margaret urged him to come to Wales as soon as possible in order to capitalise on this fund of goodwill.[17] Throughout May and June 1485 Henry struggled to raise enough ships and men to make his attempt viable, knowing that a powerful appearance would encourage others to declare themselves. Eventually, with the somewhat grudging support of the French Council, and by borrowing money on the credit of his prospects, he managed to assemble about 2,000 mercenaries, and accompanied by some 300 or 400 English exiles, set out from the Seine on 1 August. He landed at Milford Haven on the 7th, encountering no resistance, and set off via Haverfordwest to march through what is now

Ceredigion and Powys into England. His march was beset with anxieties because, in spite of the lack of opposition, he had so far recruited very few new followers, and it was only on the 12th that his worst fears were allayed when he was joined by Rhys ap Thomas with a force which just about doubled his numbers. The powerful Welshman had been as good as his word.[18] Messages of support came in from his mother, Lord Stanley, Lord Stanley's brother Sir William, and from Gilbert Talbot. The latter actually joined him with 500 men. However, the Stanleys had not moved, and without them his army looked very small to encounter the host which Richard had by them assembled against him. In the event, when the two forces encountered near Market Bosworth in Leicestershire on the 21 August, it transpired that Richard's much larger army was riddled with disaffection, and a large part of it did not engage. That, and the fact that the Stanleys turned up in the nick of time, turned the fortunes of battle Henry's way and he won a decisive victory.[19] Richard was killed in the fighting, and Henry was proclaimed as king on the field. It is even alleged that the crown from Richard's helmet was used in an impromptu coronation ceremony. The fact that the King had died childless, leaving only a nephew as his heir, meant that Henry's victory was generally accepted as the will of God, and his reign began forthwith. Within a few days he had issued letters announcing his accession, secured the person of Edward, Earl of Warwick, the fifteen-year-old son of the Duke of Clarence (and a potential rival for the throne), and set off for London. Edward was incarcerated in the Tower, and Elizabeth restored to her mother with the warmest commendations for her safekeeping. Lord Stanley and his wife accompanied the new king to his capital, where he immediately issued writs for the convening of a parliament, and fixed his coronation for 30 October.[20] In spite of his inexperience in such matters, it was essential that Henry should appear to know what he was about, and he quickly assembled a council consisting very largely of those who had served Edward IV in the same capacity. He swiftly rewarded with titles, grants and offices those who had served him in exile, or had smoothed his path to the throne, particularly his uncle Jasper, who became Duke of Bedford, and his stepfather Lord Thomas Stanley, who became Earl of Derby, but most of his councillors were drawn from those Yorkist loyalists who had rejected Richard, many of whom, like John Morton, had joined him in Brittany after 1483.[21]

Henry, meanwhile, was crowned in style. No expense was spared to make the occasion as glittering as might be, and the traditional ceremonies and rituals were strictly observed. The Great Wardrobe spent a fortune (over £1,500) on trappings for the occasion. On 27 October the King dined with the Archbishop at Lambeth, and followed this with a procession through London to the Tower, where he spent the next two nights before the ceremony itself. Archbishop Bourchier anointed him, and was assisted by the bishops of Durham and Bath and Wells. The new Duke of Bedford acted as Steward for the occasion, and places of honour were reserved for the King's mother the Lady Margaret, and for his intended bride, Elizabeth of York. Henry had made no move in the direction of marriage, partly because he did not want to make it appear that his title to the throne depended in any way upon her, and more importantly, because a dispensation would be needed because of the degree of affinity which existed between them.[22] Such a dispensation could only be obtained from Rome, and the Pope had not yet recognised him as king, so that situation needed careful and thoughtful handling. The parliament which convened on 7 November, perhaps deliberately, gave him his cue by petitioning him to remember his promise to the Lady Elizabeth, and thus reinforced his intention by the will of the estates, representing the realm of England. Henry might be newly crowned and only twenty-eight years old, but the succession was never far from his subjects' minds, and such a marriage would be an ideal way to heal the long breach between the houses of York and Lancaster. It may be significant that the petition was only offered after the parliament had declared the King's title, 'To the pleasure of All mighty God, the wealth, prosperity and surety of this realm of England', reversed the attainders of his followers, and made financial provision for the new reign. In other words it took its place in a calculated order of priorities.[23] This gave the King some breathing space, and an opportunity to get to know the young lady, whom he had probably never set eyes on, and to accustom her to the idea of wedding a man she did not know. Moreover, at the time that the parliament met, Elizabeth was still stigmatised as a bastard by an unrepealed Act of Richard III, and that had to be reversed before any question of marriage could be entered into. So there were good reasons for the delay, quite apart from the susceptibilities involved.

The dispensation was probably applied for in early December, perhaps even before the petition was received, but these things took time and in this case the testimony of eight witnesses. Realising the urgency of the matter, Pope Innocent VIII allowed the Apostolic Delegate to England and Scotland, James Bishop of Imola, to issue an interim dispensation on 16 January, just two days before the ceremony took place. Henry must have known in advance that the decision would be a favourable one, because more than two days would have been needed for the preparations.[24] Indeed the prompt arrival of Prince Arthur in September suggests that the couple were sleeping together before they were married, although no one commented upon that fact at the time. Not very much is known about the wedding itself; even the participation of Archbishop Bourchier is little more than speculation. Despite the fact that it was celebrated by chroniclers and commentators as marking the triumphant end of the feud of York and Lancaster, no proper account of it survives, and it must have been celebrated in some haste. The papal bull of confirmation was dated 2 March 1486, describing the circumstances of the Bishop of Imola's action, giving the degrees of kindred dispensed, and stating that it had been in response to the petition of the magnates and people of the realm. Finally on 23 July a decree was issued, setting out a notarial copy of the process before the Apostolic Delegate, and threatening the sentence of excommunication against anyone denying the validity of Henry's claim to the throne.[25] The full decree had taken time, but it had been worth waiting for. Not only was it retrospective in its effect, but it carried the full weight of papal recognition for his title, which was essential for the negotiations which were by then under way with other European rulers. Queen Elizabeth fell pregnant at once, and bore a son on 19 September, confirming in the eyes of all but the most recalcitrant that Henry's triumph was the will of God.

One of those recalcitrants was John de la Pole, Earl of Lincoln. John had been Richard's designated heir, but had at first made no show. Early in 1487 he fled to Flanders and countenanced (if he did not inspire) the imposture of Lambert Simnel, who claimed to be the true Earl of Warwick. Recognised and supported by his 'aunt' Margaret of Burgundy, Simnel secured a coronation in Ireland and, with a mixed band of Irish kerns and German mercenaries, invaded England in pursuit of his claim. He was defeated and captured at the Battle of Stoke on 16 June, and the Earl of Lincoln died in the battle.[26] This was the end of any immediate challenge to the King's position, and he now felt it safe to crown his queen. On 10 November he issued a commission to Jasper, Duke of Bedford, to discharge the office of Steward of England at this coronation, and the ceremony was held at Westminster on the 25th. Elizabeth was a loving and dutiful wife, and was later described as being beloved of the people 'because she is powerless'. Henry certainly trusted her, and early in 1487 transferred to her her mother's jointure. This was probably voluntary on the Queen Dowager's part, and may well have been connected with her declining health. She retired to the convent at Bermondsey with an annual pension of 200 marks, which Henry paid with every sign of filial affection until her death in 1492.[27] Elizabeth may well have been pregnant again by the end of 1487, but if so she had a miscarriage because there is no official record of her condition, and it was November 1489 before she produced a second child – a daughter who was named Margaret. Margaret's christening was overshadowed by the creation of her brother Arthur as Prince of Wales, which occurred on the 29th, and not very much is known about her upbringing. She later married James IV of Scotland and died in 1541.[28] She would have been taught to read and write, and subsequently had a reasonable command of French. These skills were imparted by tutors, but she seems not to have shared lessons with her brothers, and was spared the strict regiment of classical reading which was imposed upon them. Instead her education would have been that thought suitable to a royal or aristocratic girl, and consisted largely of piety, needlework and household management. There are some indications that she read widely, but her reading matter seems to have consisted of Chaucer, Froissart and Malory rather than anything more substantial.[29] In other words, she was trained to be a wife or consort, and her intellectual ambitions, if she had any such, would have been largely frustrated.

By the beginning of 1491 Elizabeth was pregnant again and on 28 June gave birth to her second son, who was named Henry. Whereas Arthur had been recognised as Duke of Cornwall from his birth, Henry had no title until he was created Duke of York in 1494 at the age of three. Unlike Arthur, Henry was robust child, and grew into a youth of great stature and athleticism, eventually succeeding his father as King Henry VIII in 1509.[30] At some time in 1492 a second daughter was born to the Queen, and named Elizabeth; however, she did not survive infancy, dying in 1495, shortly after the birth of a third girl, who was called Mary, and is the subject of this study.

1

THE INFANT PRINCESS

Mary was apparently born on 18 March 1495/96, according to a note in her mother's psalter which there is no good reason to doubt.[1] Like the other royal offspring she would have been put to a wet nurse until she was weaned, and then placed under the care of a dry nurse, because royal ladies did not suckle their own infants, and it is uncertain how much Mary would have seen of her mother as she left infancy behind. Arthur, as Prince of Wales, had his own household and was not normally resident in the court, but the girls, although they had their own attendants, were not similarly indulged and their nursery remained within the household, travelling with it from place to place. This involved quite a lot of movement because even the greatest palaces became insanitary after several weeks of occupation and the court seldom stayed in one place for more than a month. The main base was Eltham, but journeys downriver to Greenwich were frequent, while upriver lay Westminster, Richmond and Windsor, less often visited but still important residences.[2] Meanwhile the nursery at Eltham was washed and fumigated, ready for fresh occupancy. The children's world was circumscribed, because although there was a constant stream of distinguished visitors who came to inspect them, and they were occasionally paraded for that purpose, they would have had little or no contact with such men, and their exposure to the normal life of the court was minimal. It is unlikely, for example, that two-year-old Mary was even aware of the celebrations in London in 1497 which marked the arrival of the sword and cap of maintenance from Pope Alexander VI, which entitled her father to style himself 'Protector and defender of the Church of Christ'.³ Her own vision of God at that point would have been rather more limited. It is possible that she did remember the fire which destroyed much of Richmond Palace on 22 December in the same year, because the court was in residence at the time, and the blaze is alleged to have started in the King's apartments. It was principally the old buildings which suffered, and the fire was extinguished after three hours.⁴ No lives were lost, but the hurried evacuation may well have remained in her mind. Normally, however, trips up and down the river between Greenwich and Westminster would have been the limit of the young royals' exposure to the outside world.

Although we know next to nothing about how Mary spent her time during the first few years of her life, thanks to the survival of the Wardrobe accounts we are rather better informed about how she was dressed. Silks and damasks were issued which would have been made up into baby clothes by her attendant ladies. Stiff and wholly inappropriate for a small child as these may now appear, they would have been the normal garb for a noble infant of that period, which insisted on cramming its children into scaled-down versions of adult costume at the earliest opportunity.⁵ Blankets, bedding, napkins and handkerchiefs were also provided regularly, and ribbons of coloured silk or gold for the princesses.

At the age of three or four Mary was wearing voluminous long-sleeved dresses, with full kirtles and tight-fitting bodices, hopelessly encumbering for an active child. Play in the modern sense was clearly not on the agenda, but she seems to have grown up without any ill effects from this type of deprivation. Perhaps more suitable clothing was permitted within the confines of the nursery. By the time that she was four, in 1499, Mary had a whole collection of dresses, including purple satin and blue velvet – and eight pairs of soled shoes. Clearly she lacked for nothing which would have made her presentable.[6] Unfortunately the records are silent on how often she would have been shown off in these splendid garments. How much Elizabeth herself was involved in the rearing of her daughter is an open question. The lack of reference to her in this connection would suggest not very much. There are, for instance, only two allusions to Mary in the Queen's Privy Purse expenses for 1502. One is for twelve pence for a papal pardon during the jubilee year of 1501, which must have been a mere gesture because it is hard to see what sins a six-year-old could have committed, and the other is for 12s 8d paid to a tailor for making her a gown of black satin.[7] Apart from these there is nothing. That does not necessarily imply neglect, because her expenses may have been differently met, but it does suggest that the Queen was too busy with public and household duties to supervise the lives of her children. Nevertheless, when she died early in 1503 they all seem to have felt the loss keenly, so perhaps she had other ways of making her presence known. Some time later Thomas More imagined the dying Queen taking leave of her children; 'Adieu my daughter Mary, bright of hue, God made you virtuous, wise and fortunate', although He did not make More a very good prophet.

The person who seems to have taken her duties most seriously in connection with their upbringing was the children's paternal grandmother, Margaret Beaufort. Margaret was a woman of extraordinary toughness and determination, whose influence over her son is known to have been profound. Margaret's properties were restored to her as soon as Henry was accepted as king, and various other houses were granted to her, including the mansion of Coldharbour in London, to use when she was not resident at court. Politically sensitive wardships were conferred on her, and she was at first given the custody of the Earl of Warwick before the King decided that he would be safer in the Tower.[8] Elizabeth stayed with her in the weeks before her marriage, and she played a leading part in both coronations. In 1488 both she and the Queen were issued with liveries of the Order of the Garter, which was an especial mark of favour. No woman could be a member of that chivalric order, but this grant enrolled them as associates, and gave them a part in the Garter ceremonies. It has been remarked that her role was very similar to that which Cecily, Duchess of York, had discharged at the beginning of Edward IV's reign.[9] She frequently joined the King and Queen on their progresses, and her proximity to the royal couple seems to have been taken as a matter of course. Although she had no theological training, her piety was austere and diligent, and contributed significantly to the high moral tone which Henry liked to impose upon his court. Her education had been rudimentary. She had married at thirteen and borne her son before her fourteenth birthday. Consequently she had no Latin, nor any other language apart from French, but she was very appreciative of the learning of others, and became a notable patron of the humanists. She was particularly close to John Fisher, who became Bishop of

Rochester in 1504, and with him founded the college of St John in Cambridge, for the specific purpose of promoting the new learning.[10] It was almost certainly her influence which dictated the appointment of Bernard Andre as tutor to Prince Arthur, and later John Skelton from her favourite university of Cambridge, and these appointments in turn guaranteed a curriculum of strict classicism for both him and his younger brother, Henry. By 1500, when their accomplishments were brought to the attention of Erasmus, they were the best-educated princes in Europe. It may also have been she who insisted on them being 'bible learned' in a manner never seen before, and quite at odds with the prevailing ethos of aristocratic education. She was not, of course, a member of the Council, and politically her influence was limited, but culturally she reigned supreme. It was perhaps characteristic of her that she did not attach the same importance to the education of her granddaughters as she did of the boys. In both cases her attitude was pragmatic. Arthur certainly and Henry possibly were being trained as rulers, and for them a knowledge of history and philosophy were essential if they were to govern well. The girls were being brought up for a more domestic role, and their priorities were good appearance, piety and chastity. It was highly unlikely that either of them would find themselves in the kind of position which Margaret herself occupied. There are occasional slight signs that Elizabeth resented this intrusion into her proper realm of responsibility, but she was no match for Margaret when it came to strength of personality, and in any case the King would have it so. In spite of her royal blood the Queen was by nature passive, even submissive, so the pair appeared together in public on numerous occasions with every outward sign of harmony. Perhaps Elizabeth was relieved that so forceful a person was prepared to take over the demanding task of supervising so lively a brood, while she got on with the essential task of giving birth. However, in that respect fortune had deserted her. She may have had an abortive pregnancy in 1497, but her next live birth was of Edmund, who was born in 1499. For a while Henry had three living sons, but Edmund did not survive infancy, dying in 1500.[11] Arthur, the golden hope of both his parents, succumbed to consumption in 1502, and it was in an effort to repair that damage that the Queen again became pregnant later in that year. She died in childbirth on 11 February 1503, and the child, a daughter named Catherine, swiftly followed her to the grave. Margaret's reaction is not recorded, but she would have been sufficiently occupied in consoling her son, who was devastated by his loss.[12]

The royal nursery was at first presided over by Elizabeth Denton, but she left not long after Mary's birth to become a lady-in-waiting and was replaced by Anne Cromer, about whom nothing is known apart from her name. Unlike Arthur, Mary was given no separate establishment, but by 1501 she had her own staff of attendants, which was paid out of the Chamber account. This included a physician and a schoolmaster, along with the wardrobe keeper and gentlewomen of the chamber, but it was not large, and nothing very much is known about it – not even who the schoolmaster may have been. The King's thinking in this respect can be seen in his order of 1502 that his daughter was to be attended on the same scale as his recently widowed daughter-in-law, Catherine of Aragon, for whom an allocation of £100 a month was made, which was enough for six to eight servants – adequate for Mary, but mean for the Dowager Princess of Wales.[13] In 1498, when Margaret was nine and Mary three, a

French maiden was imported, partly to keep them company, but more importantly to teach them French by the painless method of daily conversation. Neither the age nor the name of this young lady are known, but it is reasonable to suppose that it was Jane Popincourt, who would have been about seven at that point.[14] Jane was certainly a member of the Chamber shortly afterwards, and much later created a scandal when she became the mistress of the Duc de Longueville while he was in England in 1513. At what point Jane's morals may have begun to stray is not known, but it cannot have been until about 1503, and if she had any influence over Mary at that time it has escaped the record. It is highly unlikely that the Countess of Derby would have tolerated her continued presence if she had been under any suspicion, because the princess's chastity was a jewel beyond price.

By 1499 two of King Henry's surviving children were spoken for in marriage. Arthur had been committed since 1496 to Catherine, the youngest daughter of Ferdinand and Isabella of Spain, who was a year older than himself, while Margaret was on offer to the twenty-eight-year-old King of Scots, James IV. This negotiation had been suspended in 1497 when James briefly supported Perkin Warbeck in his impersonation of Richard of York, but had been resumed two years later when the truce of Ayton was signed between the countries.[15] The former marriage took place in November 1501 and the latter in August 1503, just as soon as the parties were old enough to cohabit. Whether Henry ever considered betrothing his younger daughter as a baby we do not know, but in November 1498 there came an offer which he had no difficulty in refusing. The party concerned was Ludovico Sforza, the Duke of Milan, who was looking for allies to confront a threatened French invasion, and he sent to London a special envoy with a threefold request. Firstly he sought an alliance with England, in order to fend off the advances of Louis XII, who had picked up French ambitions in Italy where Charles VIII had laid them down. But Henry replied that he was at peace with France, and had no intention of disrupting that situation. Secondly, in order to seal the alliance, he wanted a marriage between Mary, who was then three, and his own son Massimiliano, who was about the same age. To this the King answered politely but firmly that there was no way in which he would consider betrothing his daughter until she reached the age of seven. If Ludovico was still interested in four years' time, he would be happy to give the matter serious consideration. The Duke's third request was the Order of the Garter for himself. However, it was breach of etiquette to solicit such an honour, and the King responded by pointing out that since the King of France was already a knight, it would not be possible to gratify him. 'The knights of old who bore this badge swore to be friends of friends and foes of foes', and therefore it would be impossible to admit any enemy of Louis as a member.[16] Henry loved prevarication, and kept the Milanese envoy Raimondo de Raimondi waiting almost forty days for this unsatisfactory response, by which time Raimondo had long since come to the conclusion that Henry preferred French gold to anything that the Duke had to offer. It may be significant that the Venetian report of these exchanges did not come until 1 April 1499, and the Venetians were usually well informed.[17] In fact Ludovico sought in vain for allies, not only in England but in Italy and the Holy Roman Empire as well, and was overthrown by the anticipated French invasion later in the same year. On 6 October Louis made a solemn entry into Milan, which had been conquered in a series of campaigns.

Not long after the Milanese envoy had been dismissed, Mary had an encounter which she may well have recalled later, although it is unlikely to have made much impact at the time. She met Desiderius Erasmus. The great scholar had been persuaded to come to England by William Blount, Lord Mountjoy, who had been a pupil of his in Paris, and while staying with Mountjoy in Greenwich he was taken by Thomas More to visit the royal schoolroom at Eltham. Erasmus later recalled the event:

> In the midst stood Prince Henry, now nine years old, and having already something of royalty in his demeanour, in which there was a certain dignity combined with a singular courtesy. On his right was Margaret, about eleven years of age, afterwards married to James, King of Scots, and on his left played Mary, a child of four. Edmund was an infant in arms ...[18]

Arthur was not there, having an establishment of his own, and Mary, absorbed by her game, was not much impressed by the great man. Erasmus was mainly interested in Henry, with whom he later entered into a Latin correspondence, and had difficulty in believing that the Prince's letters were really of his own composition. Mary he noted as being 'divinely pretty', but had no other comment to make. It would have been difficult for the scholar to relate to a child of that age, and there is no reason to suppose that he spoke to her at all. He had little English and Mary's French would have been rudimentary at that stage. He saw Henry as a potential patron, with justification, but there would have been no expectation of such a benefit from conversing with either of the girls, let alone one who was not much more than an infant. Although she learned some Latin as well as French,

Mary's schooling was not intellectually demanding, and may well have frustrated a girl of her natural intelligence. Only in music was she stretched, and learned to perform well on several instruments, under the guidance of professionals who are only identified in the accounts by their Christian names.[19] She also seems to have learned the techniques of composition, although nothing by her is known to have survived. Above all, like most Tudor gentlewomen, she was diligent with her needle, learning the embroidery at which she was later to excel, and probably the arts of plain sewing as well. Margaret Beaufort was a proficient apothecary, and it is likely that she transmitted some of these skills to her granddaughter, because in addition to managing the household ministering to her servants' ailments was part of a lady's responsibilities. In the event, although not learned in the sense that her nieces were later to be, Mary grew up well balanced and cultivated, possessing at least a superficial knowledge of the humanities.[20] Not enough to have impressed Erasmus, but sufficient to give her the edge over her attendants, and to convince the gentlemen of the court. We know that she did not share her brothers' schooling, and her sister would have been rather too old, so the chances are that a small group of aristocratic damsels formed a schoolroom for her, although apart from Jane Popincourt we do not know who they might have been.

King Henry VII was not intellectually trained himself, and may have felt at a loss in the company of his well-educated sons, but he appreciated that the world was changing and that his successor would need to be learned in a sense that he was not. He therefore patronised scholars and allowed his tastes to be guided by them. Knowing that expensive tastes were status symbols, he spent lavishly on buildings, jewels and magnificent hospitality. He also insisted that his whole court be splendidly attired, both the women and the men, and his daughters grew up surrounded by luxury. 'There is no country in the world,' wrote the Spanish ambassador de Puebla, 'where Queens live in greater pomp than in England, where they have as many court officers as the King.'[21] This may mean no more than that Elizabeth was indulged by a loving husband, but she certainly had a large retinue, and they were all splendidly dressed when de Puebla paid a call, which may not have been as unexpected as he believed. Mary was thus given a high standard to live up to, which explains the satins and brocades referred to in the accounts, and she grew up with a love of fine clothing which never diminished. By the time that she was about ten, with her sister married in Scotland, Mary was the third lady of the court after her mother and grandmother, and lived in some style. She may even have had her own musicians, over and above her tutors, because every member of the royal family entertained some instrumentalists, but these were no doubt paid for by her father, and would not have counted against her allowance. From 1504 onwards, Henry had his own establishment as Prince of Wales, and after his accession the Chapel Royal, which included all the musicians as well as the choristers and Gentlemen, numbered 114 men and boys and cost nearly £2,000 a year.[22] Certainly under Henry VIII, and probably under his father, the Tudor court was the finest musical centre in Europe, and Mary would have learned to dance, which she did with great enthusiasm, to the finest accompaniment available. We do not know whether she had a good singing voice, but given her brother's accomplishment in that direction, it is probable that she had.

In spite of her patronage of humanist scholars, Lady Margaret's views on the education of girls appear to have been distinctly old-fashioned. She was proud and austere, and seems not to have thought that the reading prescribed for the boys was at all suitable to a modest maiden. Latin was all very well, but it did not need to extend much beyond the offices of the church, and the works of Ovid, recommended for Arthur and Henry, were particularly unsuitable. A regime of unremitting chastity was laid down, which was all very well for an eight- or nine-year-old, but became irksome with the onset of puberty. Margaret was wedded and bedded at the age of fourteen, but for fourteen-year-old Mary, protected alike by her grandmother and by her attendants from the sexual adventures normal for a girl of that age, it must all have been rather oppressive. We do not know what she thought, but she was a lively child, and the strictly chaperoned dances which was all she could expect at court can hardly have been satisfactory, so she seems to have grown up with an unsatisfied sexual curiosity, which was blandly ignored by those about her. Ideas were changing, but not soon enough to have been of any benefit to Mary. Insofar as the old standards were laid down in writing, they were embedded in the *Ancren Riwle* and the *Garmond of Gude Ladeis*, and could be summed up as homemaking, chastity and salvation – not necessarily in that order.[23] Even Chaucer had little more to offer to the frustrated teenager of the early sixteenth century. It was not until 1523, when Mary was already a mother, that Luis Vives wrote *De Institutione Feminae Christianae* for the guidance of Catherine of Aragon. Vives believed that girls should be taught good Latin, and plenty of it, so that they might study the wisdom of the ancients. Even Greek might be appropriate, given the aptitude, but the purpose of this learning remained depressingly familiar: 'that which doth instruct their manners and inform their living, and teacheth them the way of good and holy life'. The means were enlightened, but the objective had not advanced very much beyond Margaret Beaufort.[24]

Vives, who never suggested that a woman might have the intellectual capacity of a man, was nevertheless highly controversial in his day. Many of those who wrote on the subject were sceptical of the need of girls for any academic training, and equally doubtful of the effect which such a training might have. Women were, they argued, frail by nature, both physically and morally, 'inclined by their own courage unto vice' as one of them put it.[25] In reading they would incline to that which was 'sweet' rather than to that which was 'wholesome', and classical literature would 'inflame their stomachs a great deal more to that vice'. In other words the ancient authors would 'set forward and accomplish their forward intent and purpose', giving them ideas above their naturally humble station in life. Vives by contrast believed that women had an innate tendency to virtue, which would be encouraged by such studies. His ideas were received both earlier and more sympathetically in his native Spain than they were in the north, and Catherine of Aragon had been one of the earliest recipients of these ideas. She had been thoroughly trained in the humanities, and wanted to make sure that her own daughter was similarly advantaged. So she brought Vives to England, and encouraged him to write his book. He was never actually tutor to the young princess, but he drew up a scheme of studies for her guidance, and dedicated the *Institutione* to Catherine.[26] The Queen of England was not the only royal lady with advanced ideas. Her near contemporary Louise of Savoy, who became the Queen Mother of France in 1515, went further and promoted the idea of equality in education between the sexes, a more radical notion than Catherine ever held, and one which she practised in the bringing up of her own children, with the result that Margaret of Angouleme was one of the best-educated ladies of her generation. Although Louise was practising and Vives was preaching while Mary Tudor was still in the schoolroom, no such notions were allowed to penetrate the shield which surrounded her. The reading which was prescribed for her – and we do not know exactly what it was – would have been designed to make her pious, to love good, hate evil and above all embrace chastity. 'There is nothing that Our Lord delighteth more in than virgins,' as one preacher remarked. All women were supposed to go to their husbands on their wedding nights as *virgines intacta*, and their prospects of a good marriage would be ruined if that were thought not to be the case. God, declared St Jerome, could do anything, but not restore virginity.[27] So wealth, and even royal status, paled into insignificance by comparison with chastity, and a princess, even if she were allowed to read the classics, could expect to be guarded day and night. It is therefore not surprising that as she neared the marriageable age Mary's sexual curiosity remained unsatisfied, and the changes which were affecting her body continued to be dark and uncomfortable mysteries.

Meanwhile, she had lost her mother. When Arthur married Catherine in November 1501, he had been far from the lusty swain that he was made to appear. His health had been suspect for some time, and it is probable that he was suffering from the early effects of consumption. Henry VII, however, following the fiction rather than the fact, had permitted the couple to live together from the start. This was partly because they were both legally of full age, and partly because he wanted Arthur to keep a court at Ludlow in order to reinforce the royal authority in the Marches of Wales. In spite of some adolescent boasting on Arthur's part, it is probable that the marriage was never consummated, and his health continued to deteriorate. Less than six months later, in April 1502, he died.[28] Henry was devastated, and made his own grief worse by blaming himself for allowing the couple to cohabit. Although it is highly unlikely that that had anything to do with his death, it was believed at the time that premature or excessive sexual activity could have a fatal effect upon the young. Having dutifully comforted her husband in his grief, Elizabeth then gave way to her own emotions, and promised him that the damage could be repaired. They were both young enough to try again. Sure enough, the Queen conceived promptly, but she was now thirty-six and this was her eighth or ninth pregnancy. All seemed to be going well, and after Christmas 1502 she retired, as was customary, in the royal apartments of the Tower of London. There, at the beginning of February, she was delivered of a child. Unfortunately it was not the hoped for prince, but another girl, who was named Catherine, but who lived only a few days. Elizabeth then succumbed to puerperal fever, that scourge of early modern childbirth, and also died, as we have seen, on 11 February. Henry 'privily departed to a solitary place, and would no man should resort unto him'.[29] It had been a deeply affectionate marriage, and the King was never to be quite the same man again. After lying in state for several days, the Queen's body was carried through London for burial at Westminster. 'She was a woman,' wrote Polydore Vergil 'of such character that it would be hard to judge whether she displayed more of majesty and dignity in her life than wisdom and moderation.'[30] Over 600 masses were said for the repose of her soul, as she would have wished, and she was generally mourned. We know nothing of

Mary's reaction to this bereavement. She does not appear to have attended the funeral, in spite of receiving the same mourning clothes as other members of the family, but her apparent absence may be due to the incompleteness of the records. She had not been particularly close to her mother, and may have blamed her for the strict regime to which she was subjected. However, she was barely eight at the time, and speculation is probably pointless. What we do know is that the mourning weeds were soon rejected, and that shortly after she was appearing in dark blue damask. For whatever reason she did not share her father's extreme grief, and her life must have continued much as before under the watchful eye of her grandmother.

2

THE PRINCESS OF CASTILE

Between 1502 and 1505, Henry turned his foreign policy around. Before 1502 his main concerns had been to secure a peace with Scotland and a firm alliance with Ferdinand and Isabella. The former he had achieved by the Peace of Ayton in January 1502, whereby he also undertook to marry his daughter Margaret to the King of Scots as soon as she reached the canonical age of cohabitation. The latter had been concluded by the proxy marriage of Prince Arthur with Catherine of Aragon in July 1499, and by their personal union which was solemnised at Westminster on 4 November 1501.[1] Margaret and James were married on 8 August 1503, and thereafter Scotland ceased to be a serious concern. However, with Spain it was otherwise. Arthur died in April 1502, and the question of what was to happen to Catherine became important. Ferdinand was keen to maintain the English alliance, and for that reason did not make haste to reclaim his daughter. At first Henry seemed equally amenable to continued friendship, and proposed that Catherine should be transferred to his second son, Henry, a move which was particularly favoured by Isabella. Unfortunately the Duke of York was only eleven years old, which

Mary Rose

meant that the seventeen-year-old Catherine would have to wait. However, she could wait in England, and that did not appear to pose any problems.[2] However, in February 1503 Elizabeth of York died, and after a decent interval that put the King of England himself onto the marriage market, a fact which he could not ignore, little as his appetite may have been for such an adventure. A formal treaty for the marriage of Catherine and Henry was drawn up on 23 June 1503, and ratified by Ferdinand and Isabella on 30 September. The fact that such a marriage was within the degrees of consanguinity, and was forbidden by the canon law, meant that a dispensation would be necessary, but that was not expected to present great difficulties. Indeed it would probably not have done so except that Pope Alexander VI died in August 1503, and it took his successor Julius II some eighteen months to get around to issuing it.[3] By that time Henry had gone cold on the whole idea, and complications had arisen in Spain, because on 26 November 1504 Isabella had also died. This not only removed the principal advocate of the marriage, it also created problems over the Castilian succession. Isabella's heir was not her husband, but her daughter Juana, married to the Archduke Philip of Burgundy, and if Juana's claim was upheld, Philip would secure the Crown Matrimonial of Castile, and Ferdinand's usefulness as an ally would be drastically reduced. In July 1505, as soon as he had achieved his fourteenth birthday, Henry caused his son to repudiate the marriage agreement on the grounds that it had been entered into without his consent.[4] This left Catherine stranded, because the King of England had no further use for her, and her father did not want her back in Spain, confusing the question of the succession still further. She stayed in England, unhappy and neglected.

5544

Henry, meanwhile, was hedging his bets, because in the summer of 1505 he expressed an interest in wedding Ferdinand's niece, the recently widowed Juana of Naples. In June he sent envoys to Valencia to interview her, and their report leaves little to the imagination. Her physical charms were considerable, but her financial situation was much more doubtful, and nothing came of the initiative.[5] Ferdinand expressed himself strongly in favour of the match, but it is obvious that Henry was trying to understand the Castilian situation, and the likely impact of the arrival of Philip and Juana. The King of Aragon was probably being less than honest in his desire for the marriage, because he seems to have concluded soon after that France would offer a better prospect of support than England. He made a treaty of alliance with Louis XII in October 1505, and married Louis' niece, Germaine de Foix on 18 March 1506.[6] This undoubtedly freed Henry from any lingering sense of obligation to his former ally, and left him free to pursue a new relationship with Philip and Juana. Such a relationship had begun in a sense as far back as 1496, when he had signed the so-called *Magnus Intercursus* with Philip. He was keenly aware of the importance of Low Countries trade to the economic well-being of London, and was always anxious to keep on good terms with all his neighbours. This was followed up with a meeting between the two rulers at Calais in 1500, when amid much festivity they got down to the serious business of negotiating a new treaty of friendship. This was duly signed in early June, and included provision for a twofold marriage bond. The nine-year-old Henry was to wed Philip's eldest daughter Eleanor, and five-year-old Mary was pledged to Charles, who at four months old was in no position to object.[7] How seriously these commitments were taken on either side may be doubted. Henry's was not allowed to stand in the way of his betrothal to Catherine just two years later, and Mary's was conveniently put into cold storage until the diplomatic revolution of 1505–06 brought it back to life.

No treaty of this kind would last any longer than the mutual advantage of the contracting parties, and in 1502 Philip thought that he spotted a greater benefit in a treaty with France. Because Louis had no sons, his daughter Claude was the heir, through her mother, to the Duchy of Brittany. She was not the heir to France because of the Salic Law, but no such law applied to the duchy, and it seemed likely that the personal union of Brittany with France, which had resulted from the marriage of the Duchess Anne with the French King would terminate with the life of whichever of them died first.[8] This made Claude a very desirable match, far more so than Mary, who had no such inheritance prospects. So Philip signed a new treaty of friendship and marriage with Louis, which effectively annulled his agreement with Henry. However, Louis proved equally slippery, and towards the end of 1505 renounced his understanding with Philip by bestowing his daughter upon the eleven-year-old Francis of Angouleme, who was his kinsman and next heir to the Crown of France. His desire to maintain the union of Brittany and France clearly took precedence over the prospects of the young Charles, glittering though they might be.[9] Philip had also moved on since 1502. Thanks to Isabella's death he was now King of Castile in the right of his wife, as well as Lord of the Netherlands and Burgundy, and potentially a more powerful player on the European scene than his father the Emperor. This brought him into a natural rivalry with France, and more inclined to look favourably upon a renewed understanding with England. Then on 16 January 1506, fate intervened to push him in the same direction, because in setting sail for Spain to establish his position there, a winter storm forced the royal couple to take refuge in an English haven. Some of his ships were lost, and the remainder scattered.[10] Taking advantage of this fortuitous development, Philip notified Henry of his arrival, and sought the hospitality of the English court. Although he may well have been irritated by the delay to his main plan, he was quite astute enough to play the distinguished guest, and to take his opportunity to improve relations. Juana was also given the chance to visit her younger sister Catherine, whom she had not seen since 1496, but it is not clear that she displayed much enthusiasm for the reunion. Anxious to make a good impression, Henry surpassed himself in hospitality. He sent Prince Henry, with a distinguished escort of nobles, to Winchester to welcome his royal guests, and they arrived in London on 31 January to face almost three months of parties and entertainment. In spite of her sister's indifference, Catherine enjoyed these celebrations a good deal, because they represented a welcome break from the normal tedium of her life on the fringes of the court. The ten-year-old Mary seems also to have welcomed the opportunity to enjoy herself, and may not have been indifferent to the fact that these were the parents of her one-time intended. Perhaps if she made a good enough impression, she might become again the Princess of Castile![11]

Early in February the royal guests were escorted by their host to Windsor, where Philip was entertained with some hunting in the great park, and the royal apartments were lavishly decorated in their honour, with:

great and rich beds of estate, hangings of rich cloth of gold [and]
rich and sumptuous cloths of Arras with divers cloths of estate
both of the kings's lodgings and in the king of Castile's lodging,
so many chambers, hall, chapel, closet galleries with other
lodgings so richly and very well appointed ... as I think hath not
been seen.[12]

All this generosity of course had a purpose, and served as a cover
for those serious diplomatic discussions which Philip must have
been anticipating. The King of Castile was formally invested
with the Order of the Garter, a gesture which he reciprocated
by bestowing the Toison d'Or on the Prince of Wales, and on 9
February the secret Treaty of Windsor was signed. This basically
committed Henry to the Habsburg cause in Spain. He recognised
Philip as King of Castile, and pledged himself to assist him with
military aid should anyone seek to invade his realms either in
Spain or the Netherlands. Although Philip was to meet the costs
of such assistance, this effectively gave him what he wanted, and
completed the political realignment of Western Europe. Henry,
Philip and Maximilian now stood against Louis and Ferdinand.[13]
The Emperor's inclusion was a filial piety on Philip's part,
because he was not likely to be an active player in any conflict
which might result. In return Henry secured the surrender of the
White Rose, Edmund de la Pole, Earl of Suffolk, who had taken
refuge at Philip's court in 1497. This rather insubstantial Yorkist
pretender was handed over at Calais on 16 March and promptly
disappeared into the Tower.[14] Within a few days the King of
England had also committed himself to a marriage with Philip's
widowed sister, Margaret of Savoy, an arrangement made with
the Emperor's consent. How serious he may have been about

this is not known; the lady herself was unwilling, and he seems not to have pursued it with any enthusiasm. Finally, just before he departed on 23 April, Philip authorised his agents to conclude the commercial treaty known in the Low Countries as the *Malus Intercursus* because it was so favourable to English interests. Perhaps the King of Castile thought that it was a price worth paying for so much hospitality received, but if so he had second thoughts because he never ratified it.[15]

Mary cannot have been far from her father's thoughts during these exchanges, but we have no record of what was said, or of whether the earlier suggestion of a marriage for her was followed up. We only know that no agreement was entered into at this time. Mary danced and sang for the entertainment of the visitors, and played on the lute and the clavichord, performances which attracted much admiration, and earned for her a kiss from Philip, and a place among the royal guests under the canopy of state.[16] This was no doubt a welcome break from the schoolroom, but in the majority of the adult entertainments she would have had no part. In a sense Mary was the first lady of the court, following the death of her mother and Scottish marriage of her sister Margaret, so she was allowed to present some of the prizes at the jousts or feats of arms which took place during the visit. However, she was too young to participate in the hunting which occupied the guests at Windsor, and whether she watched any of this pastime we do not know. In June 1506 the Venetian ambassador reported that an envoy had arrived to discuss a marriage between the King's daughter and 'Don Carlo, the son of the king of Castile', which certainly suggests that the topic had been discussed during the visit. Other reports in July declare that the negotiations were well advanced, but before the end of September all such plans were thrown into doubt by the unexpected death of Philip in Spain.[17] This not only raised questions as to the validity of the treaties which he had agreed with Henry, but also caused confusion in Castile. In theory he had been only the King Consort, and sovereignty remained vested in his widow Juana. However, Ferdinand succeeded in raising doubts about her fitness to rule, and eventually had her confined as a lunatic, taking over the throne himself, a move in which he was supported by a significant section of the Castilian nobility which had no appetite for an unmarried queen, however sane she may have been. In respect of the Low Countries, Margaret took over her brother's obligations, but politely declined the suggestion of a marriage with Henry, and did not ratify the *Malus Intercursus*. Instead she seems to have raised the possibility of a union between the English King and Philip's widow, who in spite of her uncertain mental health was deemed to be strong and capable of bearing sons.[18] Henry toyed with the idea, but did not pursue it. However, the suggestion of a marriage between Mary and Charles was a different matter, and was followed up vigorously. In September 1507 de Puebla wrote to Ferdinand that an ambassador from Flanders had brought such a proposal, which presumably represented an advance in the negotiations, and on 5 October he wrote again reporting not only that Margaret had written a 'very loving' letter to the King, confirming the treaties which Philip had signed during his visit to England, but that 'A marriage between the Prince of Spain and a princess of England has been concluded, and that all things … had been settled according to his [Henry's] wishes.'[19] Meanwhile, in May and June 1507, to demonstrate her arrival in the adult world, the eleven-year-old Mary had presided at the jousts and given away the prizes. This was undoubtedly a part of her political education, because she was learning the culture of chivalry in practice as well as in the schoolroom, where she seems to have been reading Christine de Pisan, Petrarch's *Griselda*, Boccaccio, and other works appropriate to her status in the court.[20]

She was being groomed as a royal bride, and on 21 December a treaty was signed between Maximilian, King of the Romans, Prince Charles of Spain and Henry VII, confirming the espousals of the young couple. This treaty was to be ratified by Charles within two months of his achieving his fourteenth birthday, that is to say by the end of April 1514. The other agreements signed by King Philip were to be ratified in the same way, but this was the one which was ultimately to matter. Another document of the same date declared that a proxy marriage was to take place within forty days of the same birthday, and that a dowry of 250,000 crowns was to be deposited with the merchants of Bruges in anticipation of that happy day.[21] When he heard this news, Ferdinand was rather less than delighted. He had been included in the terms of the treaty as a matter of courtesy, but had not been consulted. He professed himself in favour of the marriage, but wished to make his ratification dependent upon a similar union between the Prince of Wales and his daughter Catherine, a marriage which, as we have seen, Henry had repudiated in the summer of 1505. In the event Ferdinand's reservations did not matter; the treaty of perpetual peace with the Emperor was specific enough to satisfy even the English, accustomed as they were to Maximilian's slippery ways. Mary's jointure of towns in the Low Countries was to be the same as that allocated to her great aunt Margaret, Edward IV's sister, when she had married Charles the Bold, and heavy bonds were exchanged to ensure the completion of the contract.[22] Henry was delighted at having pinned Maximilian down, and at Christmas ordered 'all possible demonstrations' of rejoicing to take place in London and the other cities of the kingdom. Bells duly rang out, bonfires were lit and hogsheads of free wine distributed. However, the treaty remained unratified, and the Emperor continued to flirt with the French. It took a timely loan of 100,000 crowns and a couple of prodding missions before Maximilian finally confirmed the agreement at Brixen on 22 February 1508. Charles added his assent on 26 March, but it was not until 1 October that Margaret sent a special mission to London to complete the process.[23] She had not been a party to the original treaty, but would play a vital part in its implementation.

By this time Mary was thirteen, and it was decided to anticipate the treaty by holding a proxy ceremony at once, in spite of the fact that Charles was only eight. Given the changeable nature of renaissance politics, it was probably wise not to wait another five years for his formal ratification, which did not, in any case, come within the specified time limit, as we shall see. At this point, the Emperor made a great show of enthusiasm, and sent over an honourable embassy on 1 December 1508 to conduct the wedding. This was headed by the Sieur de Berghes, who was to act as proxy for Charles, and Jean de Sauvaige, the President of Flanders. They were sumptuously received, first at Dover and later by the King himself at Greenwich. Ten days later, on 17 December, Mary was married, and the event was recorded for posterity by Pietro Carmeliano, Henry's Latin Secretary:

... the king's highness being under his cloth of estate, the ambassador of Aragon and the Lords Spiritual sitting on his right hand downward, and my Lord the Prince [of Wales] with the other Lords Temporal sitting in like wise on the left hand, and the said ambassadors [of the Emperor] sitting directly before his Grace, the President of Flanders proposed a proposition containing the cause of their coming, which was for the perfect accomplishment of all things passed and concluded for the said amity and marriage at the town of Calais ...[24]

The Archbishop of Canterbury then began the proceedings with an address in Latin on the dignity of holy matrimony, and the significance of this particular union from which 'many great and notable effects' were intended to spring. De Sauvaige replied in kind, and Berghes then joined the Princess on the dais and avowed the loyalty and undying affection of the absent bridegroom. He repeated his authority to represent the Prince in the vows which were to be exchanged, and Mary took his hand, repeating in French the formula:

I, Mary, by you John Lord of Berghes, commissary and procurator of the most high and puissant Prince Charles, by the Grace of God Prince of Spain, Archduke of Austria and duke of Burgundy, hereby through his commission and special procuration, presently read, explained and announced, sufficiently constituted and ordained, through your mediation and signifying this to me, do accept the said Lord Charles to be my husband and spouse, and consent to receive him as my husband and spouse. And to him and to you for him, I promise that henceforth during my natural life, I will have, hold and repute him as my husband and spouse, and herby I plight my troth to him and to you for him ...[25]

The whole ceremony was conducted *per verba de praesenti*, in words of the present tense, and therefore should have constituted a complete and binding marriage. The use of proxies was common in royal weddings, and was not deemed to detract from the binding nature of the exchange of vows. However, it could be argued – and was to be later – that the absence of subsequent consummation made this less than a perfect union. That was debateable in the canon law, and Charles's status as a minor also called its legality into question, which was why the original treaty had specified confirmation after he had reached the canonical age of consent. Meanwhile Berghes placed a gold ring on the middle finger of her left hand, and 'reverently' kissed her, while the court musicians played the company into the mass which followed. There then ensued a state banquet and three days of jousting, dancing and other festivities.[26] Mary watched the sports from a richly adorned gallery, but was allowed to work off some of her natural exuberance in the dance. She appears to have enjoyed her enhanced status as Princess of Castile, but it is not obvious that it made any difference to her normal lifestyle, which continued to be that of a pupil and dependent.

Carmeliano's tract, entitled *Solennes ceremoniae et triumphi*, was translated into Castilian and Catalan, and John Stiles, Henry's ambassador in Spain, presented a copy to King Ferdinand, who appears to have been less than delighted. He was no doubt looking ahead to the time when Charles might hold the Crowns of Spain, and Henry's successor would have a legitimate interest in Castile through the right of his sister. It may be significant that Gonsales Fernandez of Cordoba, the Great Captain of Castile, was alleged to be delighted by the news, 'and many with him'.[27] No doubt their agenda was rather different from the King's. On

18 December, Charles wrote to his bride, as etiquette required, addressing her as 'ma bonne compaigne' and sending her three 'goodly and right rich' jewels as tokens of his affection. The first of these was a balas ruby, garnished with pearls, which actually came from the Archduchess Margaret; the second, from Maximilian, was a brooch with a large diamond; and the third, from Charles himself, a monogrammed ring garnished with diamonds and pearls, which was inscribed *Maria optimam partem elegit que non auferetue ab ea* – an ironic comment on what was to follow.[28] These were personal gifts, but the ambassadors had also brought other jewels with them as collaterals for Henry's loan to the Emperor, notably the 'Rich lily' or fleur de lys, which was an arrangement of gold and precious stones weighing no less than 211½ ounces troy. Years later, in 1529, it was to be returned to Charles V as a part of the settlement following the Peace of Cambrai, when it was described as being so heavy that it required a pack horse to carry it.[29] The ambassadors departed, just before Christmas, loaded with rich gifts which expressed Henry's satisfaction with the results of his diplomacy, and Carmeliano lauded his employer to the skies:

> Rejoice England, and to thy most noble victorious and fortunate sovereign lord and king give honour, praise and thanks … Thy flourishing red rose be so planted and spread in the highest imperial gardens and houses of power [that] all Christian regions shall hereafter be united and allied unto thee, which honour until now thou couldst never attain.[30]

In the last few months of his life, Henry was at peace with the world. With France, and with Ferdinand, relations were uneasy but peaceful; with Scotland, the Empire and the Low Countries, friendly. However, there was unfinished business, notably the marriage of his son, and it may have been for that reason that on his deathbed he urged Henry to wed his long-neglected ex-fiancée, Catherine – if, indeed, he said any such thing. He had been anxious to secure Ferdinand's support for Mary's marriage to Charles, and this may have been intended as a late bid for that.[31] Catherine herself had never ceased to believe that such would be her destiny, and she remained in England partly for that reason, not pressing her father for a return to Spain. Her marriage also became the focus of much earnest prayer, and her belief in it became an aspect of her religious life. Ferdinand meanwhile decided to take advantage of her place in the English court, and gave her an enhanced purpose in life by accrediting her as an additional ambassador during the summer of 1507. He was at that time dissatisfied with the efforts of his regular representatives. Dr de Puebla had fallen out with Catherine, and lacked the status to sustain his mission, although his information continued to be useful, and his replacement, Don Gutierro de Fuensalida, was an aristocratic bungler who got everything into a mess.[32] So the use of Catherine in this connection was not only shrewd but wise. It gave her an additional entrée into the royal presence, and improved her English remarkably. It also gave her some much-needed resources. She was nothing if not frank with her father, and on 9 March 1509 she wrote to him complaining of the impossibility of working with Fuensalida and of the unkindness of the King, 'especially since he has disposed of his daughter in marriage to the Prince of Castile, and therefore imagines he has no longer any need of your Highness'.[33] She may have been wrong about Henry's attitude towards Ferdinand, but it did not greatly matter as the King died on 21 April, and the political situation was transformed, along with her own prospects.

Henry VII died at Richmond, and there his body lay in state until 8 May, when it was borne in solemn procession to St Paul's, where the obsequies commenced with a sermon by Bishop Fisher of Rochester, and a requiem mass was sung. The following day the cortège proceeded to Westminster, where the interment took place and the officers of his household cast their broken staves of office into the grave. The total cost of these ceremonies was about £8,500, and formed a fitting send-off for a king who, although not loved, was deeply respected and very rich.[34] Henry's will made suitable provision for his younger daughter, setting aside £50,000 for her dowry and marriage, over and above the costs of her transport into the Netherlands, 'furnishing of plate, and other her arrayments for her person, jewels and garnishings for her Chamber'.[35] This was to be equally available if the marriage to Charles was not completed, because he was only too aware of the conditions which still applied to that union. In that event, Mary was to be at the disposal of Henry VIII and his Council, although the hope was expressed that 'she be married to some noble Prince out of this our realm', because he was only too aware of the factional implications of a domestic marriage. In the meantime, she was an adornment at her brother's court. At about this time she was described to Margaret of Austria as having

the most gracious and elegant carriage in conversation, dancing, or anything else that it is possible to have, and is not a bit melancholy, but lively. I am convinced that if you had ever seen her you would not cease until you had her near you. I assure you that she has been well brought up, and she must always have heard Monsieur [Charles] well spoken of, for by her words and manner, and also from those who surround her she lives him wonderfully. She has a picture of him … and they tell me that she wishes to see him ten times a day, and if you want to please her you must talk of the Prince. I should have thought that she had been tall and well developed, but she will only be of medium height, and seems to me much better suited both in age and person for marriage than had heard tell before I met her …[36]

However, for the time being the consummation of this union was on hold, and Henry VIII was more concerned with his own glory than he was with the well-being of his sister. As soon as the regulation days of mourning were past, the court threw itself into an orgy of celebration for its magnificent new sovereign. Jousts, feasts and dances followed one another, and for the time being policy remained in the hands of his Council, which continued substantially as his father had left it. There was soon another cause for rejoicing, because Henry married his sister-in-law Catherine in a low-key ceremony at the Franciscan church in Greenwich on 11 June. Whether he did this out of respect for his father's dying injunction, or out of any desire to mend fences with Ferdinand, we do not know. It seems more likely that he simply fancied her, because although at twenty-four she was six years his senior, she was very attractive and not otherwise committed.[37] Her commission as an envoy had come to an end with the old king's death, and he may well have given her some indication of his intention before that. Catherine was triumphant, because this represented the answer to all her anxious prayers during the lean years of her exclusion, and she was soon to write to her father of the 'endless round' of celebrations in which the young couple were engaged. Fuensalida was astonished, because several days after Henry VII's death he was still being told that the young king was free to marry where he chose – and no indication was given as to where that choice might fall.[38] On 21 June, just ten days after their wedding, the King and Queen rode into London to resounding acclamations, to take up residence at the Tower, as was customary before a coronation. The following day twenty-six 'honourable persons' joined the royal couple for dinner, and on Saturday the 23rd were made Knights of the Bath. The coronation ceremony itself was held at Westminster on 24 June, which was Midsummer's Day, with Archbishop Wareham presiding. The Queen was crowned alongside her husband, and both the city of London and the nobility of England strove to be worthy of the occasion.

> If I should declare [wrote the chronicler Edward Hall] what pain, labour and diligence the tailors, embroiderers and goldsmiths took to make and devise garments for lords, ladies, knights and esquires and also for the decking, trapping and adorning of coursers, jennets and palfreys, it were too long to rehearse; but for a surety, more rich, nor more strange, nor more curious works hath not been seen than were prepared against this coronation.[39]

As soon as the ceremony was over, the entire company retired for a magnificent banquet in Westminster Hall, and for a tournament which lasted until dark. Many days of jousts and feastings followed, in which the King's young companions distinguished themselves, and Henry himself spent long days in the saddle, following his hawks and hounds. He did not, however, take part in the tournaments himself, apparently heeding the advice of his Council that it would be a disaster if he should be injured (or worse still killed) in an accident to which the sport was prone. Catherine was a happy onlooker, no doubt sharing the Council's reservations, and Mary appears to have been her constant companion. In spite of the ten-year difference in their ages, they were firm friends, and the younger woman no doubt took advantage of the opportunity to ask discreetly about the pleasures of the marriage bed.

Henry, meanwhile, was set on fighting the French. This was partly the natural bellicosity of youth, because his head was full of chivalric dreams and he idolised his predecessor Henry V, but also partly a shrewd calculation. In the first place he knew that the quickest route to the glory which he craved was via the battlefield, and that Louis XII was getting old and might well lack the stomach for such an encounter, but he also knew that his nobles were fretting against his father's regime of peace. They still saw their service to the Crown primarily in military terms, and the younger ones in particular had never seen service of that kind.[40] If he was to avoid domestic trouble once the round of entertainments had ended, he would be well advised to give them some congenial employment. Consequently although he renewed his father's treaty with France, he made it clear that this was on the advice of his Council, and he insulted the French ambassador by declaring that Louis dared not look him in the face.[41] He knew perfectly well, however, that he could not fight a war against France single-handed. He needed allies, and that was where Ferdinand, Maximilian and Charles came in. The former was gratified that his daughter's marriage had at last taken place, and kept up a friendly but non-committal correspondence with his son-in-law, but Maximilian proved even harder to pin down. There was no reason to suppose that the marriage agreement would not be fulfilled, but Charles seems to have been unimpressed by the eulogies of his bride which reached his ears, muttering (with some exaggeration) that he needed a wife and not a mother.[42] How the fifteen-year-old Mary reacted to being described in such a fashion – if she ever found out – we do not know. Henry did his best to keep the treaty in mind, in the summer of 1511 sending a force to assist the Archduchess in her small war with the Duke of Gueldres, reminding the 'noble lady' that there was 'a communication hanging … between the young Prince Charles [Margaret's nephew] and the lady Mary his sister'.[43] In the meantime he had signed a new treaty with Spain in May 1510, which effectively annulled that with France which had been renewed only two months earlier. Divisions in the Council were now becoming obvious, and it was time for the King to assert himself. His assistance to the Archduchess was a step in that direction.

The European situation was also moving in his favour. The League of Cambrai, which Julius II had formed against the Venetians in 1508 was breaking up, as the focus of the Pope's anxiety moved from Venice to France. In 1510 he began to prepare a new league, directed this time against Louis, and the King of France responded by calling a council of the French bishops to make traditional Gallican noises. He then went further and attempted to call a schismatic General Council to meet at Pisa in May 1511, for the specific purpose of deposing Julius.[44] The council never met, but the result was a full-on confrontation between the Pope and the King of France, and the former now began to call his alliance a 'Holy' League, designed to defend the unity of the Church. This League was duly signed at Rome in October 1511, the original signatories being the Pope, the Emperor and the King of Spain. Within a month Henry had persuaded his Council to abandon a neutral position, and to take advantage of the opportunity which the League presented. War with France was decided upon, and was formally declared at the end of April 1512.[45] Preparations had been under way for some time, and Henry's navy was at sea within days of the declaration being made. At the beginning of June, in accordance with a prearranged strategy, the Marquis of Dorset also led an expeditionary force of some 12,000 men to Guienne, to co-operate with Ferdinand's proposed invasion of southern France. The result was a fiasco, because the King of Spain provided none of the logistical back-up which he had promised, and when Dorset proposed to advance from San Sebastian to attack Bayonne, Ferdinand declined to co-operate. Instead he used the English presence as a cover for an attack on Navarre, a move in which the English had no interest. Without action and marooned in a hostile environment, Dorset's men became sick and mutinous; the council of officers was rent with quarrels, and the Marquis himself became ill. Eventually, in October, the surviving men commandeered ships and returned to England, a sad remnant of the proud host which had set forth only four months earlier.[46] Dorset had no option but to return also, and might have expected a rough reception. However all Henry's anger was directed against Ferdinand, who had so conspicuously failed to honour his obligations. For the time being the alliance held, but it was greatly weakened.

One of the results of this failure was that it became easier for the King to keep his alliance with Maximilian separate from that with Spain, and to maintain friendly relations with the elusive Emperor. He even advanced him 100,000 crowns with which to hire Swiss mercenaries on the understanding that Maximilian would invade France as a part of his obligation to the League. However, at the end of 1512 he had done nothing, and it was not until 5 April 1513 that a further treaty was signed, binding the Emperor (in return for another 125,000 crowns) to make war upon Louis at the head of 30,000 men. As a result of this, when Henry himself arrived in Picardy at the head of an Army Royal in July 1513, Maximilian did actually join him in the campaign, although with far fewer men than he was committed to.[47] Meanwhile Margaret had been doing her best to keep his attention focussed on the marriage, which she saw as offering a more binding commitment than any treaty of friendship. During the summer of 1509 she persuaded Charles to send a jewel as a further token of his affection, and Mary sent him a ring in return. By the end of the year she had suggested a visit to the Low Countries to enable her to meet her intended husband and to learn something of German fashions.[48] This did not happen, but in February 1510 she persuaded the Emperor to appoint a gentlemen-in-waiting to her. This gentleman did not apparently come to England, but in the autumn of 1511 she tried again, this time sending a Fleming named John Cerf over to serve her. Henry accepted this initiative and gave Cerf an annuity until such time as the marriage was consummated, which he was clearly still expecting to be in the near future.[49] He was not alone in that expectation. Margaret was puzzled by Mary's failure to respond to her invitation, but did not think that that affected the contract, and Erasmus wrote on 6 February 1512, 'happy is our Prince Charles to have such a spouse. Nature never formed anything more beautiful, and she excels no less in goodness and in wisdom ...' Over a year later, on 13 April 1513 Mary wrote a letter to Margaret, which she signed as 'Princess of Castile', and it was being rumoured at that time that Henry would bring his sister with him when he invaded France later in the summer.[50] The Princess seems to have believed these rumours herself, because in the letter mentioned to her 'bonne tante' she expressed the hope that she would learn of Flemish fashions and would be able to introduce them in England. However the Army Royal arrived at the end of July, and Mary was not with it. The victory celebrations which followed the capture of Therouanne on 24 August were conducted without her, much to Margaret's regret. However, once Henry had returned to England she did succeed in extracting from him a joint declaration that the marriage would take place before 15 May 1514 – in other words within the forty days of Charles's fourteenth birthday, as specified in the original treaty.[51]

Meanwhile the war effort stuttered. In March 1512 Julius II had stripped Louis of his title to France, and conferred it on Henry. This was less significant than might appear, because it was made clear that the grant was conditional upon the King of England actually conquering France, which he was in no position to do. In fact it was a mere gesture, intended rather to express the Pope's deposing power than to bring about any change in the military situation. More importantly, early in 1513 Ferdinand signed a one-year truce with Louis, and thus effectively withdrew from the League. At about the same time, in February 1513 Julius II died, and his successor Leo X had no desire to continue his predecessor's feud with the French. There was even talk of a defensive alliance between Spain and France, which could have brought Ferdinand into the war on the other side. That did not happen, but by the time that Henry and Maximilian were conducting their campaign in Picardy in the late summer, they were doing so without Spanish support, and the possibility of a southern front against France had evaporated.[52] At the same time James IV of Scotland intervened on the French side. He had no particular quarrel with his brother-in-law, but the opportunity created by the King's absence in France seemed too good to miss. His adventure came to a bloody and fatal end at Flodden on 9 September, but not before it had caused considerable anxiety to the regency government of Catherine of Aragon, who had been left to 'mind the shop' in Henry's absence.[53] All these considerations meant that when a nuncio from the new pope arrived early in 1514 to persuade him to make peace, he was disposed to listen. He was also moved in that direction by his new chief adviser, Thomas Wolsey. Wolsey had made his mark in 1513 when he had organised the logistics of the Tournai campaign, and had managed to get men and supplies where they were needed in time to be of use – no mean achievement in sixteenth-century conditions. He was hugely efficient, and the King was most impressed, but he was also disposed to follow the Pope's lead and argue for peace in the difficult circumstances of 1514. Consequently although arrangements for the marriage were pressed ahead, and by the middle of February had got as far as the lodging provision for Mary's train, an air of uncertainty was beginning to prevail on both sides. On the 25th of that month Margaret inquired rather belatedly what would happen to the English succession if Henry were to die without a son. Perhaps she was unable to believe that the King would risk giving his sister to a Habsburg, who notoriously extended their territories by matrimony.[54] At the beginning of April the Prince's health was giving cause for concern, and Mary was warned to be careful because all the arrangements were in the hands of his entourage. At the end of April the ever-optimistic Margaret wrote to the Emperor that all the preparations were complete, and that Mary would be arriving on 2 May.[55] Where she got her information from is not clear, because on 4 June she received a letter from Henry, excusing his sister, and wanting both the timetable and the place altered. He regretted that the marriage could not go ahead as planned. On 23 July the King was reported to be angry with the Emperor for the delay over the marriage, but by that time it was effectively dead. Since early April Henry had been toying with the idea of sealing a peace with France by marrying his sister to Louis, and on 30 July she formally renounced her engagement to Charles, citing as a reason the fact that he had not ratified the treaty of which it had been a part within two months as had been agreed in 1508.[56]

The Prince's reaction to this rejection is hard to gauge. Although he had written to her in December 1513 as 'votre bon mari', that appears to have been out of a sense of duty (or perhaps on instruction) rather than from any real conviction. Whereas Mary's professions of affection for him were numerous, he is not known to have reciprocated. Ferdinand, similarly, although he professed himself in favour of the marriage was privately gratified because he did not want any move which would strengthen his grandson in his claim on Castile. He still had hopes of issue by Germaine de Foix. Maximilian was affronted, but he had only himself to blame, because he had blown hot and cold on the project, and was seeking delays right up to the last minute. The person who was most genuinely upset was Margaret of Savoy, who had worked tirelessly to bring the marriage about, seeing it as the surest way to cement an alliance between England and the Low Countries. However, Margaret was at odds with her Council over this issue, most of the latter favouring a settlement with France. Henry, got in first, and was self-righteous about his choice. He had been deceived by both Ferdinand and Maximilian, and felt perfectly entitled to take his revenge. He did not see, he told the Venetian ambassador, 'any faith in the world save in me, and therefore God Almighty, who knows this, prospers my affairs.'[57] He might also have added that he had found in Thomas Wolsey a diplomat whose skill and lack of scruple more than made up for his own innocence, but it was typical of him that he should reserve the credit for himself.

3

THE POLITICS OF MARRIAGE

On 9 January 1514 Anne of Brittany, the queen of Louis XII, died. In a very important sense she had failed in her royal duty, because she had borne him no son, but only two daughters, Claude and Renee, the former of whom was her heir in respect of the Duchy of Brittany. At that time the failure of male heirs was always deemed to be the fault of the woman, and deeply though Louis may have mourned her, he still believed himself capable of repairing that omission. St Thomas Aquinas had written:

> As regards the individual nature, woman is defective and misbegotten, for the active force, the male seed, tends to the production of a perfect likeness in the masculine sex; while production of woman comes from defect in the active force …[1]

In spite of his age (he was fifty-two) and uncertain health, he was therefore keen to marry again. Meanwhile, in order to secure the personal union of Brittany and France he married Claude to his prospective heir and kinsman, Francis of Angoulême, in a quiet ceremony at St Germain-en-Laye on 18 May. The twenty-year-old Francis, who was a notorious womaniser, was consoled for his sweet-natured but physically unattractive bride by being able to assume the title of Duke in the right of his wife. In June 1515 Claude made over her rights in Brittany to her husband, and he continued to administer the duchy after her death in 1524 in the name of their son Francis, who was a minor. It was not until August 1532, and with the consent of the estates, that he finally issued the decree which annexed the duchy in perpetuity to the Crown of France.[2] If Louis had succeeded in begetting a son in the winter of 1514/15, and the child had lived, Francis would therefore presumably have remained Duke of Brittany and the institutional union would never have taken place. Such is the importance of royal fertility in the politics of the renaissance.

Meanwhile the allied war effort had petered out. At the New Year of 1514 Henry was talking of his new campaign, preparing his navy and collecting munitions. Then, at the end of February, suspicious rumours began to emerge from both Spain and the Low Countries that both Ferdinand and Maximilian were thinking of opting out. A week or two later these fears were confirmed. Ferdinand had signed another truce with France, not only in his own name, but in those of the Emperor and the King of England also.[3] He justified this extraordinary action with a story about an elaborate conspiracy by the Pope and others to drive both him and Maximilian out of Italy, and alleged that the initiative had come from the Emperor. Maximilian would, he claimed, have consulted Henry as a matter of course before adding his name to the signatories. Only the Emperor had done no such thing, and the King was left bitterly chagrined by this act of betrayal.[4] For the time being, Henry continued to talk as though he intended to fight on. It would be, he alleged, 'a very great dishonour' to hold back because his allies had defected. Troops were mustered and warships put to sea. In June an English force ravaged the French coast near Cherbourg, in revenge for French attacks on Brighton earlier in the year, and as late as the beginning of August a league was entered into with the Swiss for putting an army into the field against France at English expense.[5] Yet there was an air of unreality about these warlike posturings, because at the end of January Gianpietro Caraffa had arrived as a papal nuncio in England in an endeavour to persuade Henry to make peace. His reception was at first ambivalent, but he was assisted in his efforts by the Duc de Longueville, who under the guise of negotiating his own ransom became an unofficial representative of the French King. He had been taken prisoner at the Battle of the Spurs but was always treated more as guest than a captive and was allowed a good deal of freedom. His efforts for peace were ably seconded by Fox and Wolsey, who, in spite of the strenuous opposition of some members of the Council, gradually persuaded the King of the validity of their point of view.[6] Wolsey was only slightly exaggerating when he claimed later, 'I was the author of this peace.'

Having freed himself from the hostility of the Empire and Spain, Louis was anxious to bring the English conflict to an end, and was kept well informed of developments in London. In early April it was being reported in Paris that he had two aims in mind; the first was to seal peace with England by marrying the King's sister and the second was to match his younger daughter, Renee, with Ferdinand, Maximilian's ten-year-old grandson.[7] This appears to be the first mention of his sister in this context. The idea obviously appealed to Henry, who had become increasingly exasperated by the Emperor's efforts to put off Mary's union with Charles, and at the end of May Louis wrote to Henry as though the deal was done. On the 31st he thanked the King for agreeing to the match, expressing the pious hope that the union would be 'of great benefit to Christendom'.[8] Leo X, anticipating success, had sent Henry his sword and cap of maintenance, which the latter received in a ceremony at St Paul's on 21 May. Just before the treaty was signed, Leo sent word to Wolsey that he would like to be included, since the idea of marriage had been his in the first place. Presumably he had planted the suggestion in Louis' mind, from whence it was communicated to Henry via Longueville. On 7 August what was clearly a long period of detailed bargaining was brought to an end, when the treaty of peace and friendship was signed, committing Mary to a marriage with Louis, and Louis to the payment of a million gold crowns at the rate of 50,000 a year. Her dowry was to be 200,000 crowns, which the King presumably intended to take from the 250,000 crowns which had been deposited at Bruges for just such a purpose. Tournai was to be retained by England, and Scotland was included in the treaty. Mary was to be delivered to Louis at Abbeville at her brother's expense.[9] The treaty, which was not popular in England because of its implications for trade with the Low Countries, was proclaimed in London without any sign of celebration.

Margaret was mortified, and so was Charles, in spite of his share in the responsibility for what had happened. He taxed his councillors with having deprived him of a desirable bride, and their response was equally mortifying. They pointed out that the King of France was not only his elder, but was the most powerful king in Christendom; and since he was a widower, was entitled to pick the most eligible woman to be his queen.

His response, according to a Venetian report, was to observe chillingly that they had plucked him because he was young, 'but bear in mind for the future I shall pluck you'.[10] He was to be as good as his word. Henry, on the other hand, was delighted. He had secured peace with honour in the retention of Tournai, which had been one of his principal war aims, and in communicating the tidings formally to the Pope, expressed the hope that England and France together would be able to protect the interests of the Holy See in Italy. Mary, who by this time was nineteen, does not appear to have been consulted, or if she was, expressed no recorded opinion. The news can hardly have come as a surprise to her once she had repudiated her contract to the Archduke. She was in no position to bargain with her brother, and in any case the prospect of being Queen of France was irresistibly attractive. As Marino Sanuto later noted, 'The queen does not mind that the king is a gouty old man … and she herself a young and beautiful damsel … so great is her satisfaction at being Queen of France …'[11] She may already have realised that her tour of duty was not likely to be protracted. Meanwhile Louis was not disposed to wait; he issued his proxy to the Duke of Langueville on 8 August, and a week after the treaty was signed, on 13 August, the wedding took place *per verba de praesenti* at Greenwich. Henry and Catherine led the English delegation, which consisted of all the dignitaries of the realm as well as Mary and her ladies. The French were represented by Longueville, and by two of Louis' ministers who had been sent over especially for the negotiations, John de Silva the President of Normandy and the soldier Thomas Boyer. Papal envoys were also present, but the Spanish and Imperial ambassadors absented themselves, as a gesture of disapproval.[12]

Archbishop Warham presided, assisted by Wolsey as Bishop of Lincoln, and a number of other prelates, and he opened the proceedings with a Latin address on the sacredness of marriage – very similar to that which he had used at Mary's previous proxy union in 1508. On this occasion de Silva replied in the same language, but confined himself to intimating his master's intentions. Longueville's authorisation was then read by the Bishop of Durham, and the proxy marriage followed, the Duke holding Mary by the right hand and speaking Louis' vows in French. Mary duly responded, the ring was placed on her finger, and the ritual kiss given. It must have been uncomfortably reminiscent of her wedding to Charles, but nobody commented to that effect. What followed, however, was different, because once the ceremony was over Mary changed out of her bridal gear into a discreet nightdress and lay down on a bed which had been provided in an adjacent room. Longueville then bared one leg and lay down beside her for long enough to enable his leg to encounter her body, whereupon Warham, who together with others had witnessed this odd encounter, pronounced the marriage consummated.[13] What the lady may have thought of this play-acting is not recorded! When she was dressed again the whole company proceeded to High Mass, Longueville walking with Henry and Mary accompanied by Catherine. After mass, a banquet followed, with music and dancing which went on for about two hours, during which both the bride and her brother demonstrated their exceptional talents, to universal applause. Mary was showered with congratulations and wedding presents from all over Europe, the most splendid of which came from her husband. Two coffers of plate and jewels arrived under the conduct of the Sieur de Marigny. One of these jewels was a diamond 'as large as a man's finger', with a pendant pearl 'the size of a pigeons egg', which was known as the Mirror of Naples and was valued at 60,000 crowns. Louis was nothing if not generous.[14] Part of Marigny's brief was also to familiarise the new queen with the customs of the French court, and he brought with him an artist, one Jean Perreal, whose job it was to paint a portrait of Mary and to advise on the planning of her wardrobe. The news from France was that Louis longed for her coming, and that may well have been true, but his letters to her at this time are stilted and conventional, probably dictated to a secretary. In reply she was diplomatic and correct, but no warmer in tone. It was a political marriage in every sense of the term.

The one person who was unfeignedly pleased was Henry VIII, because it put him one step ahead of his former ally, Ferdinand. Having been betrayed three times by the King of Spain, Henry was thirsting for revenge, and this marriage gave him the opportunity. It was even rumoured at the end of August that he was planning to leave his present wife, on the grounds that she was his brother's widow and consequently that he could have no children by her.[15] Nothing came of these rumours at this time, but relations between the royal couple were certainly chilled by his hostility to her father. Ferdinand was under no illusions as to what the Anglo-French entente might mean for him. Only Margaret of Savoy, preoccupied with her own concerns, thought that he might favour it as being a blow against the Emperor, with whom his relations were hostile. It was certainly unpopular in Flanders, and Sir Edward Poynings, writing to Wolsey from the Low Countries on 7 September, expressed concern about the security of Tournai because it depended for its supplies upon the goodwill of the local people.[16] Nothing, however, was permitted to disrupt the preparations for Mary's departure. Oaths for maintaining the treaty of peace were exchanged on 14 September, and on the 23rd an embassy was instructed to escort the Queen as far as Abbeville, where she was scheduled to meet the King about the end of the month. The Duke of Norfolk headed this mission, and he was accompanied by several of the Lords of the Council, including the Marquis of Dorset and the Earl of Worcester. The only slight shadow cast on these proceedings was the prudent English insistence that if Mary outlived her husband and returned to England, then the cost of her journey to Abbeville was to be refunded and her personal possessions returned.[17] On the French side her jointure was generous, equal in income to that received by Anne of Brittany, amounting to some 300,000 crowns, and a second proxy ceremony was held. This took place in the church of the Celestine Order in Paris on 14 September, when the Queen was represented by the Earl of Worcester, only the gesture of consummation being omitted! The following day Louis bound himself to the payment of the million crowns provided in the treaty, under penalty of excommunication for default.[18] Bearing in mind the promises which had been made and broken in the past, Henry and Wolsey now felt that they had every cause for satisfaction.

Mary's own preparations had been equally thorough. In addition to being a guest at many entertainments and celebrations in her honour, she had put together a personal wardrobe which cost her brother about £43,000, much of it in the French fashion, thanks perhaps to Perreal's advice. Liveries for her servants, the trappings of her chapel, and the possession of Great and Privy Seals all proclaimed her royal status.[19] On 22 September Louis left Paris to journey to Abbeville for their meeting, and on the

28th a tournament was held in her honour, but still she did not come. This was partly due to the foul weather, which all the glitter of her cavalcade could not alter. She left London on the 29th, accompanied by the King and Queen and, according to Lorenzo Pasqualigo, four earls, 400 knights and barons, and all their ladies travelling in great wagons. In spite of the weather the Queen of France looked quite ravishing; her equal 'was not to be found in England' in the words of the enthusiastic Venetian.[20] Meanwhile the storms made assembling the fleet which was to accompany her exceptionally hazardous, and one ship, the *Great Elizabeth*, a 900-ton hulk which the King had recently purchased from Lubeck, was wrecked near Sandgate with heavy loss of life. Nevertheless a fleet of fourteen 'great ships' was assembled at Dover to escort her crossing, and on 2 October a lull in the gales persuaded the King that it was safe for them to set off. They bade farewell to Catherine at the Castle, and Henry walked with his sister down to the waterside. It was at this point, as she later reminded him, that the King had promised to let her chose her second husband for herself if, as they both suspected, Louis might not last very long.[21] Meanwhile, having embarked, the journey proved exceptionally hazardous because they were caught in mid-Channel by a fresh storm which scattered the convoy, dispersing its ships along the coast from Calais to Ostend. Only four, including the one in which the bride was travelling, succeeded in making it to the official destination, which was Boulogne. However, having gained the harbour, the Master was unable to dock her, and instead ran her aground, leaving his seasick passenger to be conveyed ashore in a rowing boat. Eventually Mary was carried through the breakers by Sir Christopher Garnish, a knight of her household, and arrived drenched and wretched at the dock where a royal reception awaited her.[22] It is to be hoped that the Duke of Vendome and the Cardinal d'Amboise were sufficiently sympathetic to her wretched plight. The ceremonies were at all events cut short so that she was able to change into dry clothes. Gradually, over the next few days, the scattered ships arrived, and her wardrobe could be reassembled. It transpired that only a minimum of plate and property had been lost in the wreck of the *Elizabeth*, and the main damage inflicted by the storm was psychological. For a day or two it wrecked Mary's self-confidence, and was later recalled by the superstitious as being an ill omen for the marriage, which lasted barely three months. On Thursday 5 October she reached Montreuil, 24 miles from Boulogne, where she was able to spend a couple of days recuperating at the hospitable home of Madame de Moncaverel. On the 7th she was able to set out, with dignity restored, on the 25-mile journey to Abbeville, where her destiny in the shape of Louis XII awaited her with what patience he could muster.[23]

At each stop along the way she was greeted with pageants and eulogies, which must have caused her to forget the miseries of the crossing. At Montreuil she was escorted into the town by a delegation of dignitaries, led by Francis of Angoulême in his capacity as Governor of Picardy, and welcomed with a flattering song, praising the peace between England and France. As their procession entered it was entertained with a number of pageants at intervals along their route, some classical and some biblical, but all symbolic of Mary's forthcoming marriage – Perseus and Andromeda, Solomon and the Queen of Sheba, the Virgin and the Annunciation.[24] Like her brother, Mary loved these manifestations of loyalty. She had seen many similar on the streets of London, and never seemed to tire of them. In this context, their therapeutic effect was remarkable. After this, the journey from Montreuil to Abbeville was taken with becoming dignity, until in the early afternoon she was met by Francis of Angoulême, who had ridden ahead to warn Louis of her coming. He hinted darkly at a surprise that might be awaiting her, and late in the afternoon it turned up in the form of Louis himself, theoretically out with his hawks, who had chanced upon her party, greatly to his own surprise! He should not have seen her until the official reception, but his curiosity got the better of him, and this 'coincidental' encounter was his way of circumventing the strict etiquette of such matters. Nobody was deceived, least of all Mary, but honour was satisfied.[25] Louis had taken the trouble to find out what his bride was wearing, so that he could appear in a matching outfit. He duly appeared, riding a magnificent hunter, caparisoned in gold and black, and Mary, pretending to be taken aback by her royal visitor, doffed her hat and prepared to dismount from her palfrey, but he would permit no act of homage, so she blew him a kiss from the saddle. Unfamiliar with this English custom, he nevertheless returned her gesture then threw his arms around her neck 'and kissed her as kindly as if he had been five and twenty'. If she was surprised by this reaction, Mary was too well bred to show it, and they chatted together for a few minutes, after which he returned to Abbeville by a different route. Nothing must detract from the honour of her solo entry.[26]

The Duke of Norfolk had organised this as a ceremonial procession, led by fifty esquires. There then followed the lords, barons and ambassadors, splendidly clad and riding two by two, and the heralds and trumpeters, led by Garter King of Arms and Richmond Herald. Two liveried grooms leading spare palfreys came ahead of the princess, who rode alone, and was followed by about thirty female attendants, some mounted and some conveyed in gaily decorated wagons.[27] The remaining wagons, carrying her Wardrobe equipment followed behind, and the handsome royal litter, empty on this occasion, wherein she sometimes chose to travel. Bringing up the rear were two hundred archers, on foot in three companies. Before this entourage reached the town a delegation from Abbeville joined them, consisting of the mayor, chief justice, magistrates and clergy, escorted by liveried soldiers, which preceded them in their march and brought the total number in the procession to between two and three thousand. Unfortunately before they reached their destination a sharp shower of rain necessitated a change of apparel for some of the dignitaries, including Mary, who rode into the town in a dress of stiff gold brocade and under the protection of a canopy borne by four of Abbeville's officials.[28] Whether they volunteered for this duty or not is not on record! The citizens greeted them with amazement. Never before had they been treated to such an ostentatious display of wealth as the English exhibited on this occasion. One commentator explained that he could only express himself in superlatives 'for the reality exceeds my description, to the great glory of this Queen'.[29] On the outskirts of the town, at the church of Notre Dame de la Chappelle, she transferred from her palfrey to the litter, as more becoming to her dignity, and entered Abbeville through its great gate at about five o'clock in the afternoon, not long before dark at that time of the year. She was greeted by a salvo of artillery and the efforts of a hundred musicians. Un-dampened by the returning rain, the decorated streets were interspersed with several pageants, elaborately prepared in her honour, and showing the familiar mixture of classical and biblical themes.

In the centre of the town the procession dispersed, the local men returning to their homes and the English to the lodgings which had been prepared for them. Mary heard mass at the church of St Vulfran, and paid her homage to its patron saint, before being escorted to her first official meeting with the King. This took place at the Hotel de la Gruthose, and was dignified with all the ceremony of a state reception. It was not, however, prolonged, and the Duke of Norfolk having carried out the formal presentation, Mary was taken by Claude, the King's daughter and the wife of Francis of Angoulême, to her apartment in the Rue St Giles, which was actually an annexe to the King's quarters.[30] Claude, who was only a few years younger than her stepmother, seems to have been immediately attracted to this dazzling English beauty, who had so many of the qualities which she herself lacked. She was a good-natured soul, and jealousy never entered her mind. That evening a state banquet was given by Louis, and a grand ball followed hosted by the Duke and Duchess of Angoulême. In spite of what must have been a very long and tiring day, Mary delighted the company with her charm and poise. The omens for the marriage, it was generally decided, were very good. However, that night a fire consumed a substantial part of the lower town, and although this was not permitted to interfere with the King's amusements, some who were not of the court, decided that maybe the omens were not so good after all. Fortunately the loss of life was small, but many houses were burned and families lost their scanty possessions.[31]

The following morning, which was 9 October and the feast of St Denis, Anne and her entourage were early astir. The wedding ceremony was set for nine o'clock in the great hall of the Hotel de la Gruthose, just across the garden from her lodgings. The procession would be short, but if possible it had to be more magnificent than that of the previous day. This meant that, having broken their fast, the English lords and ladies had to spend a great deal of time on their apparel and appearance. Mary's gown was of gold brocade, cut in the French fashion and trimmed with ermine. She was overloaded with jewels, partly out of deference to French taste, partly to display her brother's wealth, and accompanied by a dozen ladies of her personal staff, all splendidly dressed but taking great care not to outshine their mistress. Twenty-six knights headed her brief entrée, followed by heralds and musicians, although the latter had little time in which to display their talents. Mary walked between the Duke of Norfolk and the Marquis of Dorset, who were to give her away in the name of Henry VIII, and she was followed by a miscellany of the ladies who had accompanied her to France for just this purpose. 'If the pomp of the Most Christian Queen was great yesterday at her entry ... it was yet greater at her wedding,' as one impressed spectator reported.[32] Louis, meanwhile, and his guests were waiting for her in the hall. The King, dressed in gold and ermine to match his bride, was actually outshone by some of his nobles, who had stopped at nothing to be more splendid than the English. One courtier's gown was alleged to have cost 2,000 crowns (more then £400), because a Frenchman's wealth was measured by the costliness of his attire, just as the Englishman's was measured by the weight of the gold chain which he wore round his neck. Some of the latter were claimed to be so heavy that they encumbered their wearer's movements.[33] As the English entered the great hall, the King doffed his bonnet, and the Queen dropped him a deep courtesy, whereupon Louis kissed her and seated her beside him on the dais under a canopy borne by four of the greatest peers of France. Somehow the King managed to find among her jewellery the room to clasp another necklace around her neck, which consisted of a diamond and a ruby valued, as the Earl of Worcester later claimed, at 10,000 marks, almost as much as the Mirror of Naples. Whether all these jewels were given to the Queen *ex officio*, or whether they were personal gifts was later to be a matter of great controversy, but for the time being the spectators were duly impressed by his generosity.[34] The wedding then proceeded, performed by the Bishop of Bayeux, who also sung the nuptial mass, and the royal couple then communicated, sharing the wafer between them. Once the marriage was performed, after another kiss and another courtesy, Mary was escorted back to her own quarters to prepare for the state banquet which was to follow.

For this purpose the King and Queen were again separated, he presiding over his lords in his Privy Chamber, while she sat at the head of the 'ladies table' in her own apartments, an arrangement which must have taken her aback because such was not the custom in England, where the lords and ladies dined together. That same evening there was another ball at the Hotel de la Gruthose, with the whole court supping, dancing and 'making good cheer'. However, at eight o'clock the proceedings were terminated by the ceremonial bedding of the royal couple. This was something which Louis by all accounts had been looking forward to immensely – so much so that he had difficulty in keeping his hands off her, even during the formalities of the day. The bed was duly blessed, and the bride was led to her fate by the ever-solicitous Claude. What she thought of the prospect, no one asked or wanted to know.[35] The following day by custom she remained in seclusion, while Louis 'seemed very jovial and gay'.

One reporter reckoned from his face that he was 'very much in love', and he claimed to have 'crossed the river' three times in the course of the night. All this is reminiscent of Prince Arthur's boast in similar circumstances, except that Louis was not an adolescent.

One of the dignitaries who had so far been conspicuous by his absence from these events had been Charles Brandon, Duke of Suffolk. He had been kept back, because Henry had a special mission in mind for him, and probably did not want him too closely associated with his sister, with whom his name may already have been linked. Instead he was sent across in mid-October, ostensibly to represent the King at Mary's coronation, which was scheduled for 1 November, and to help organise the ensuing tournament, but really to propose a meeting between Louis and Henry at some time in the following spring to co-ordinate a strategy against Ferdinand.[36] This might take the form of a joint campaign for the recovery of Navarre, which the King of Spain had seized in 1512, or, far more ambitious, a bid by the King of England for the Castilian succession in the right of his wife. The possibility of such a claim had been raised about eight years earlier, when Henry VII had been contemplating the newly widowed Juana as a possible wife. It could be argued that Juana's subsequent incapacity (if that was taken seriously) had devolved her claim upon Catherine, and that Henry had a duty to pursue it.[37] The King was so anxious for revenge upon his former ally that the incongruity of such an action at a time when relations with his wife were strained does not seem to have occurred to him. The idea was probably impracticable, and if Louis poured cold water on it, as he was very likely to do, Suffolk was to ask for his suggestions for an appropriate form of joint action. The

French King pretended to be impressed by his brother's zeal, and played Suffolk along, but in truth he was interested only in a campaign for the recovery of Milan. Henry's assistance in such a action would be welcome, but was not what Suffolk had in mind, and since that campaign was due to start in March, he did not make much progress in arranging a meeting either. April was suggested, somewhere between Calais and Boulogne, but nothing firm was agreed. Ferdinand's ambassador in England was gratified by these tidings when they reached him, but did not deceive himself into thinking that they made much difference to the bad relations between Henry and his master.[38] He compared himself with a bull 'at whom everyone throws darts', and the King of England to a colt in need of a bridle. Ferdinand, however, was in no position to apply such restraint, and Louis, who could have done so, was now unlikely to try.

Suffolk had his first audience with the King at Beauvais on about 25 or 26 October. Louis had travelled there with Mary, who was with him at the time of Brandon's reception, but his gout was troubling him, and he received the Duke lying down, the Queen sitting beside him.[39] Fortunately the King was well enough to travel the following day, and they set off again for Paris, a distance of some 50 miles. Suffolk, as an accredited ambassador, followed as a member of the court, although whether he got any opportunity for further conversation with Louis is not recorded. In each town they passed through, the Queen exercised her ancient prerogative of freeing the prisoners, which must have caused headaches for the local magistrates, although it made her popular with the people. They also passed the travelling time talking about the King's forthcoming Italian expedition, on which his wife became keen when he promised to take her to

Venice. It was not very often that royal ladies got an opportunity to accompany their menfolk on campaign.[40] By the time they reached St Denis, just outside Paris on the 31st, Louis appeared to have forgotten all about his gout, and was reported to be in fine fettle. The first two days at St Denis being All Saints' Day and All Souls' Day, were passed quietly in religious observances, and the King proceeded to Paris. Mary, by custom, was not permitted to enter the City before being crowned, and that ceremony was duly performed in the abbey church on 5 November, witnessed not only by the whole travelling court, but also by the King and numerous lords and ladies who had ridden out from Paris for the occasion, including the Duke of Suffolk and his companions who had travelled with Louis in order to discuss the setting up of the tournament which was to follow the coronation.[41] The actual crowning was a relatively simple event, performed by the Bishop of Bayeux, who invested her with the ring, sceptre and rod of justice. She was then conducted to a throne set in the sanctuary, where she heard high mass and received the sacrament. All this while Francis held the heavy crown over her head, lest its weight should prove too much for her. Once the ceremony was over the whole company joined the King for dinner, after which Louis left again for Paris to make quite sure that everything was in place for the Queen's entry, which was to take place on the following day.[42]

Below the surface, however, the relationship was not quite as harmonious as it appeared. On the morning of 10 October, the day after their wedding, Louis had dismissed many of his wife's English attendants, including her Chief Gentlewoman, Lady Jane Guildford. The reason for this was partly political – a French queen should be attended by French servants – but also partly personal. He felt that Lady Guildford was interfering in his relations with his wife, and this may have been justified insofar as she was Mary's chief confidante, and had been engaged as a kind of chaperone. Mary was mortified, and on 12 October wrote to her brother, lamenting that she had been left 'all alone', and commending Lady Guildford to explain the circumstances. On the same day she wrote to Wolsey, begging him to find some means whereby her Chief Gentlewoman could be reinstated.[43] Both these letters demonstrate the skill which she had acquired in this medium, and do not lay any of the blame for what had happened upon Louis. They both made soothing responses, but neither of them did anything directly to remedy the situation, although Wolsey did suggest to Suffolk that he might raise the issue with the King. Henry clearly felt that Louis knew his own business in such matters. Nor was Mary's plea entirely justified, because although the men and several of the ladies in her household had been sent packing, a core of English gentlewomen remained in her service, including Mary Boleyn and her sister Anne, who seems to have joined her from Margaret of Savoy's court at some time between her wedding and coronation.[44]

Mary's entry into Paris was an affair of the greatest magnificence. Despite the miserable November weather, the citizens had decked the streets with lilies and roses, some in silk, others painted upon arras, or on the giant billboards which marked out the route. Paris was one of the great cities of Europe, far larger than London, where all kinds of people mingled in a violent and turbulent environment, where learning, brigandage and trade rubbed shoulders. It was in English eyes a centre of vice, of whoredom and of murder, and Mary must have shared her countrymen's prejudices. Nevertheless all such thoughts were set aside as she enjoyed the pageants which the Parisians had organised in her honour. The first was at the St Denis gate, by which she was bound to enter the medieval walled city, and consisted of a ship in full sail, complete with real mariners climbing the rigging. Ceres and Bacchus were at the helm, symbolising the wine and corn trades of the city. The allusion was to Mary's crossing the Channel, and peace was the main theme.[45] The civic and university dignitaries met her at this gate, and escorted her to the Palais Royale, where the King awaited her. At the same time a choir sang songs of welcome.

> Noble Lady, welcome to France
> Through you we now shall live in joy and pleasure,
> Frenchmen and Englishmen live at their ease,
> Praise to God who sends such a blessing …[46]

Many of these verses were written by the humanist Pierre Gringore, who was appointed to make the official record of the entry, and he presented her with a handsome souvenir programme, lavishly illustrated. Mary had chosen to show herself to the best advantage, and was riding in her litter, wearing a crown studded with diamonds which had been made for the occasion, and preceded by Francis together with the dukes of Alençon, Bourbon and Vendôme. On the way from the St Denis gate she was also met by a delegation of the French clergy, thought by one optimist to number 3,000, but probably only a fraction of that number.[47] The second tableau showed a fountain playing, out of the bowl of which grew lilies and roses, lovingly entwined, while the third represented Solomon and the Queen of Sheba, in overt reference to Louis' alleged wisdom. Passing on to the church of the Holy Innocents, she was confronted by a scaffold bearing a figure of God the Father holding a large heart over images of the King and Queen. The fifth tableau, however, was the most ingenious, because it showed a walled city, enclosing a garden wherein grew a bush, and out of the bush sprouted an enormous rosebud which ascended by means of hidden machinery to a balcony whereon grew a lily of equal size. When the rosebud had completed its ascent, it opened to reveal a damsel, who recited the most complimentary of all Gringore's verses, comparing Mary to the 'rose vermeille', which had grown in the gardens of Jericho. This rose featured in many contemporary romances, and signified that to Parisians their king's bride was love incarnate.[48] Moving on to the Chastellet, she was confronted by the images of Justice and Truth, and by an orator who compared Louis to the sun and Mary to the moon. Finally at the Palais Royale itself there was a double stage showing the angel of the annunciation addressing the Virgin Mary in a thinly veiled reference to hopes of an heir, while rustic shepherds sang of the Mary of heaven and the Mary of earth. It was late in the afternoon before the Queen, who was bearing up remarkably well, arrived at Notre Dame for a reception prepared by the University, where after mass she was welcomed by the Archbishop of Paris. At about six, she returned from Notre Dame to the Palais Royale for the obligatory state banquet at which, unsurprisingly, she is alleged to have fallen asleep and been borne off to her rooms.[49] Louis, not as robust as he would like the spectators to believe, had long since retired from the fray. It had been a very long day, and it was only after a suitable rest for all concerned that the celebratory tournament began on 13 November. Mary was now wedded, bedded and crowned as Queen of France.

4

MARY AS QUEEN OF FRANCE

The afternoon following their strenuous night, on 7 November, the royal couple retired to the Hotel des Tournelles, where they rested until the great tournament in the Queen's honour, which began on the 13th. It would be difficult to say which of them was in more need of the respite. The tournament was Francis's idea, and had originally been intended as a friendly encounter between English and French nobles to celebrate the royal wedding at Abbeville. However, it was decided that so exciting a spectacle deserved a grander setting, and so it was deferred, taking place eventually after Mary's coronation and entry into Paris in the splendour of the capital city.[1] It also lost some of its original purpose, becoming instead a great renaissance spectacle, and a trial of strength between the nations. In assuming the aspect a great sporting encounter, like a modern football or rugby match, it developed a slightly sinister side, because it became Francis's intention to use the encounters as a means of demonstrating his own skill, and hopefully lowering the colours of the English jousters, at that time reputed the finest in Europe. Local interest was intense, and patriotic pride became engaged, so that it assumed an overriding importance in the long calendar of celebrations. Francis was responsible for the French team, and took it upon himself and the other nine 'challengers' to meet all the English 'answerers', both on foot and horseback.[2]

The English, for their part, were equally concerned for their team's success, realising perfectly well what Francis was about. Their representatives were chosen by Henry, who must have regretted that Louis' incapacity meant that he was unable to take part himself, because in the circumstances for him to have appeared would have been an abuse of hospitality. The team was led by the Duke of Suffolk and the Marquis of Dorset, and consisted of Sir Edward Howard, Sir Edward Neville. Sir Giles Capell, Sir Thomas Cheyney, Sir William Sidney and Sir Henry Guildford. All of them were expert lancers, and Suffolk had the reputation of being the finest in Europe (after King Henry, of course).[3] The list had been set up in the Parc des Tournelles, and large stands erected for the spectators, who were expected to be numerous and partisan. The whole court was there. Louis, troubled with recurrent gout, reclined on a couch, with Mary and Claude supporting him. Unfortunately it rained remorselessly, and ten days were needed to get through five full days of fighting. The procedure was complicated, because each participant was required to run numerous courses over three days; these were the jousts proper and consisted of individual combat on horseback with spears. However, these courses were followed by fighting on foot with swords, and by a general melee, in which many knights, organised in groups, engaged simultaneously. Altogether over 300 men took part, and there appear to have been a few fatalities which 'were not spoken of'.[4] In the midst of this organised chaos, public interest was focussed on the principals, Francis and his brother-in-law the Duke of Alençon on the French side, and Suffolk and Dorset on the English.

On the first day Alençon distinguished himself by running ten courses, and shattering a spear in each, but it was Suffolk who carried off the day's honours, running no fewer than fifteen courses, thirteen of them as challenger, which was the more demanding role. Remarkably, there appears to have been only one death, although we are told that several horses were slain, presumably by misdirected lances. On the second day also, Suffolk received the most commendation, actually unhorsing his opponent (a very difficult feat to accomplish) in three successive rounds. These bouts were fairly clinical, but the melee which followed was rough. Dorset wrote later that the fighting was as furious as he had ever experienced. He and Suffolk, he explained, had

> put our aids thereto because there was no nobleman to be put unto us, but poor men of arms and Scots, many of [whom] were hurt on both sides, but no great hurt, and of our Englishmen none overthrown nor greatly hurt …'[5]

The climax was reached on the 21st, when the courses on foot began, fighting at the barriers. Because he had injured his hand, Francis felt unable to take part, but so arranged matters that Suffolk and Dorset, whom he described as his 'aides' for the whole tournament, were set to fight alone against all comers. By elevating them to this place of honour, he seems to have hoped to bring about the Englishmen's defeat, and so to reduce the prestige which they had gained from the jousting of the first two days. If so, he miscalculated, because Suffolk was victorious in all his encounters, including one with an enormous German who had been infiltrated into the ranks of the French challengers specifically to humiliate him. The German was immensely strong, and came at him fiercely, so that the Duke was almost beaten down. However, he was also relatively unskilled, and did not know how to take advantage of his opportunity. Suffolk rallied, and defeated his opponent, pummelling him about the head until the blood gushed out of his nose.[6] The unfortunate fellow was immediately removed before his identity could be discovered. Far from being diminished by this encounter, the Englishman's reputation was enhanced, and Francis became jealous. Dorset withdrew after losing his spear, but his place was taken by his nineteen-year-old brother, Lord Edward Grey, who also fought with distinction, overthrowing another giant – only this time a legitimate Frenchman! Only in their accoutrements did the French clearly excel. Francis, the Duke of Bourbon and the Count of St Pol all appearing in stunning armour, changing their tabards each day in a rich variety of colours – purple velvet and cloth of silver. By comparison the English were soberly clad, each man displaying a cross of St George on some part of his apparel.[7] There were clowns and trick riders to enliven the scene between bouts, and the crowd obviously enjoyed the spectacle, in spite of their disappointment at the English success. Suffolk and Dorset both wrote to Wolsey after the event, being suitably modest about their triumph; news of that, Suffolk alleged, would best come from others.

Meanwhile, Brandon's mission had been more than a response to Francis's challenge in the lists, because he had also been entrusted with a secret mission to Louis XII. This was secret because there were divisions in the English Council over the desirability of a French alliance, and Henry had so far acted upon his own initiative. The 'bedchamber crisis' over the sacking of Jane Guildford had brought this to the surface, because Suffolk blamed his rival the Duke of Norfolk for this development, claiming that Norfolk, who was in France at the time, had sanctioned it in order to weaken the Anglo-French friendship, which he distrusted.[8] There was no reason to suppose that this was so, but Brandon hastened his journey to Paris, to conduct his business with the King before the Howards could stop him – as he alleged. His business was to suggest to Louis a meeting between the kings in the spring of 1515 to concert a strategy against Ferdinand of Aragon. Hence the need for secrecy, because if the Howards had gained information to that effect, they would undoubtedly have informed the Queen, and thus warned the King of Spain. In spite of his lack of diplomatic experience, and his preoccupation with the forthcoming tournament, this mission was reasonably successful. He secured Louis' agreement to the meeting, and even began to put some possible strategies in place. He also succeeded in delaying the Duke of Albany's passage to Scotland, which Henry would have regarded as an unfriendly act, given the delicate state of politics in that kingdom and his sister Margaret's role in them.[9] Louis thought well of his efforts and expressed the opinion to Henry that 'no prince christened hath such a servant for peace and war'. The Marquis of Dorset thought that his diplomatic mission had been at least as fruitful as his appearance in the lists, which was commendation indeed.[10] After the tournament and its accompanying celebrations, Suffolk returned home, to be warmly welcomed by Henry, and by Wolsey, who was the true architect of the Anglo-French alliance, and in view of the King's reaction, his opponents in the Council kept a low profile for the time being.

The day following the tournament, 24 November, was marked by a banquet given for the Queen at the Hotel de Ville by the University of Paris. This signalled the end of the court season, and on the 27th the King and Queen removed to St Germain-en-Laye for a three-week break before returning to Paris for Christmas. At the dinner there were many speeches, and the orators competed with one another in their flattery of the Queen of France, and of the coming together of the kingdoms, with France being given the benefit of the comparisons. No king of France, it was alleged, since the days of Clovis, had ever been killed in battle, exiled or murdered by his own people – a clear allusion to the fate of Edward II and Richard II of England, which was a country 'naturally prone to revolution'.[11] Mary's husband, it was implied, was more secure than her brother, a hint that the Queen was too diplomatic to take exception to. She may also have been too pleased with the adulation to notice, because such a crowd had gathered around the banqueting hall that the official party had been unable to enter by the front door. Instead they had been obliged to make a detour via the porter's lodge and the back stairs. Once inside, she was received by the elite of the City and the University, and treated to a meal of the utmost magnificence. No action or gesture on her part was unobserved, and she earned special commendation for asking that a portion of the specially prepared dessert should be sent to the royal nursery at Vincennes for her four-year-old stepdaughter, Renee.[12] One observer, who was not inexperienced in such matters, declared that he had never seen so many distinguished guests so sumptuously attired at any comparable occasion.[13] The politics of the court were complicated at this juncture by the King's attitude. That he admired and respected Mary is obvious, and she used that favour to help the Duke of Suffolk in his negotiations, because he lacked not only experience but also subtlety, which it was the Queen's job to present to her husband as 'plainness', a virtue which he appreciated. So successful was she in this that Louis came to favour the Duke above his own cousin Francis, whose ambition he obviously distrusted. During these weeks Mary's behaviour won plaudits all round, except for Francis's family, who could not stand her. She also flattered his Council by discreetly seeking their advice as to how to deal with her husband. As Suffolk reported she wanted to know

> how she might best order herself to content the king whereof she was most desirous, and in her should lack no goodwill, because she knew well that they were the men that the King loved an trusted …[14]

Louis was pleased at the pains she was taking, and Henry and Wolsey were delighted to receive such positive reports. On the eve of her departure for St Germain, Dorset declared that she 'continued her goodness and wisdom', and consequently increased in favour both with the King and with his Council. She was showing an acute political sensitivity, and a maturity and discretion well beyond her years, because she was only nineteen at this time.

The King chose St Germain for the court's retreat because it was near to Paris, and because (although he would not admit it) he was finding travel both painful and fatiguing. He seems to have intended enjoying some hunting, but was too sick to indulge in such a strenuous pastime. Part of the time he was confined to bed, and his wife sat by him, becoming daily more accustomed to the role of sick-nurse.[15] Nevertheless they managed to return to the Hotel des Tounelles in December, whereupon Louis took to his sickbed permanently, and began to prepare for the end, which he realised could not be long delayed. The great household continued to function with apparent normality, and Christmas was duly kept, but without any of the festivities normally associated with the season. Meanwhile Mary sat by her husband's bedside and talked to Francis, or rather he talked to her. She felt that he showed insufficient concern for his father-in-law's situation, and rather too much for hers, and although his behaviour was outwardly correct, she began to be disturbed. His conversation was sophisticated, and interspersed with personal observations that alarmed her, so that she began to feel that he could become a problem if (or rather when) Louis' protection was removed. She confided her anxieties by letter to both Dorset and Suffolk, and may have been prompted to take some of the French Council into her confidence in case it should be necessary at some time in the future to restrain the Duke of Angoulême's ardour.[16] It was well known in the court that Francis was of an amorous disposition, and considered himself irresistible to women. If he had been less conceited, her off-putting responses would have been sufficient to deter him. Whether he would have been prepared to cuckold his liege lord is another matter, but for the time being Mary's best defence lay in absolute loyalty to her husband. She could not, however, afford to alienate her admirer, who for all his innuendos was gracious and witty, and when Louis died, he would be king. It would be an exaggeration to say that he could then dispose of her as he thought fit, but his position would obviously be much strengthened, while hers would become weaker.[17]

Gossip circulated about the King's sickbed, most of it unflattering to the Queen, who was given singularly little credit for her continence. Much of it probably emanated from the anti-English faction at court, which was led by Louise of Savoy, but it is hard to trace to its source. There was clearly another side to the popular perception of her beauty and graciousness, because as represented in these stories, she was flirtatious, light-headed and irresponsible, 'giddy in six languages' as one author put it. She is supposed to have regarded her marriage as a joke, and the Italians in particular circulated salacious stories about her, even before Louis' final illness deprived him of all capacity to please her. One contemporary historian, Robert de la Marck, Seigneur de Fleuranges, put the derogatory case succinctly. 'The king,' he observed, 'did not feel very strong, because he had desired to be a pleasing companion with his wife, but he deceived himself, as he was not the man for it …'[18] He had abandoned the strict diet which his doctors had prescribed for him, and they warned him that if he continued he would die of his pleasure. It is from these stories that the image of a flirtatious and impetuous Mary derive. In fact during Louis' last illness she behaved with admirable restraint and discretion, and Henry and Wolsey were well advised of the fact. If it had not been so, Henry, who was something of prude, would have made his displeasure known, and the Queen's position would have become even more precarious. The records do not say very much about Louis' last weeks, and the traditions are probably deceptive. They represent the King as abandoning all restraint, indulging in rich foods and late nights in an effort to charm his youthful bride. Louise of Savoy, who was prepared to believe anything to the discredit of the royal couple, recorded in her journal that 'ces amoureuses noces' had been fatal to him.[19] There may have been an element of truth in all this, because overindulgence and unaccustomed activity, both of which were features of his attempts to please her, would probably have hastened his death. However, to blame the Queen for this seems altogether irrational, and on the other side of the coin, his marriage had undoubtedly revived his wish to live. The Earl of Worcester, who had remained behind when his fellow ambassadors had returned home at the beginning of December, wrote to Wolsey that he 'hath a marvellous mind to content and please the Queen'. Apart from banning Jane Guildford and Jane Poppincourt from his wife's entourage he had been the very model of a solicitous husband.[20]

Christmas was quiet at the French court in 1514, because the King was growing progressively weaker, and his death was clearly only a matter of time. On 28 December he rallied his fading energies to write to his 'good brother' the King of England. It was a letter full of expressions of contentment with his wife, who

> has hitherto conducted herself, and does still every day, towards me in such a manner that I cannot but be delighted with her, and love and honour her more and more each day; and you may be assured that I do, and ever shall so treat her as to give both her and you perfect satisfaction ...[21]

Clearly none of the defamatory rumours which were circulating had reached Louis ears, or if they had, then he had treated them with the scorn which they deserved. His letter went on to praise the Duke of Suffolk, commending him for his 'virtues, manners and good conditions' which deserved the highest respect. Happy indeed is the king who has such servants! It was to be Louis' last effort, and three days later he was dead.[22] Mary, who was clearly not with him at the end, is alleged to have fainted at the news. Whether she did or not, as a childless royal widow she now faced an uncertain future, and much would depend upon the support which she received from England. For the time being she had to wait at Cluny until it was determined whether or not she was pregnant by her late husband. She herself was sure that she was not, but it was necessary to be as certain as the medical science of the period permitted, because the future of the French monarchy might depend upon it.[23]

Meanwhile it was an established principal that the King never dies, so Francis succeeded Louis without a break, and immediately began to make his dispositions as king. This was not unconstitutional and would have become so only if Mary had born a son, and Francis had refused to step down.[24] That remained a hypothetical possibility for about a month, but no one took it very seriously, and Francis was duly and solemnly crowned at Rheims on 25 January. Although not in theory obliged to do so, he had by then agreed to honour Louis' obligations, including his friendship with England, and accepted responsibility for his predecessor's debts. On 2 January he had confirmed the members of the Parlement of Paris in their places, and did the same with the other sovereign courts. Over the next couple of weeks he confirmed most of the other officers who were in post throughout the kingdom, and made new appointments to the positions of Chancellor and Constable, both of which were vacant at the time of his accession. The former post, which had been empty since 1512, was filled by Antoine Duprat, the President of the Parlement of Paris, and the latter by Charles III, Duke of Bourbon, the King's most powerful vassal.[25] The big gainer by the regime change was however the new King's mother, Louise of Savoy, who was given the Duchy of Anjou and all the money obtained from the confirmation of office holders, who of course paid a fee for their recognition. This was bad news for Mary, because the new Queen Mother regarded her, as we have seen, with deep suspicion, seeing her as vamp who had her claws into her son, which was a total misrepresentation of the situation. Louis was buried at St Denis on 12 January 1515, but the Queen did not emerge from her seclusion to attend the ceremony. By custom she remained at Cluny, and wore the traditional white which was the royal mourning of France. For this reason she was known thereafter as 'la reine blanche' – the white queen. She had been married just eighty-two days, and the period of mourning was forty days, so the designation was not an unfair one.[26]

Meanwhile, she was exchanging letters with Henry and with Wolsey. Anticipating Louis' demise and her own incipient widowhood, the latter had written to her on 1 or 2 January, warning her to be careful in everything she said or did, and in no circumstances to entertain suggestions for her remarriage. This was scarcely advice that she needed, and on the 10th she replied with some indignation, 'I trust the king my brother and you will not reckon in me such childhood …' She had conducted herself honourably and with great discretion since her coming into France, and trusted that no reports to the contrary had reached England.[27] What reports Wolsey had heard we do not know, but the problem now was to retrieve Mary, and as much of her property as might be feasible. With this in mind, he advised the King to send the

Duke of Suffolk back to France as his special envoy to negotiate her repatriation, and the Duke arrived in Paris on 31 January. He saw the Queen the same day, and immediately reported formally that she wished to come home 'as shortly as may be'; she could, he said, 'never be merry' until she saw her brother face to face. She begged to be excused from writing personally as she had a toothache, which was probably a result of the stress she was under.[28] Difficulties were to be expected, because although Louis' councillors had confirmed that in the event of her widowhood she would be at liberty to return to England 'with her servants jewels and effects', and that the French would reimburse the costs of her travel to Abbeville, there remained the question of her dowry. This could be offset against the million crowns which Louis had acknowledged that he owed the King of England, provided that Francis was willing to accept that debt. There was also the problem of the jewellery which the late king had so generously given to her. Had he bestowed these upon her as his queen, in which case they should remain to her successor, or as personal gifts, in which case she was entitled to take them with her?[29] The question of the travel expenses had already been resolved before Suffolk's arrival, to the tune of £1,470, and this relatively small success boded well for the outcome of his mission, but he and his colleagues, Wingfield and West, expected to have to bargain hard for the greater sums. The situation was complicated by Francis's unwillingness to let her go. This was not because he found her attractive (although he may have done so) as because she represented a major political asset. A beautiful royal widow, not yet twenty years old, was obviously ripe for remarriage, and Francis was very unwilling to surrender that advantage to the King of England. As Sir Thomas Spinelly reported to Henry VIII on 6 February, the Dukes of Savoy and Lorraine were already being proposed, and although Mary was rejecting all such overtures, as long as she remained under his control she was vulnerable.[30] Francis seems to have been particularly concerned that once she was back in England, Henry would revive the marriage with Charles of Ghent, which had been abandoned in the previous July, and which he would have been forced to interpret as a hostile move. It was for that reason that he was prepared to welcome the news that she had secretly bestowed herself on the Duke of Suffolk. As late as 10 February, the Duke was still reporting to Henry that his sister would be married to the Duke of Lorraine, but he also reported that inventories of her goods, her wardrobe, jewels and stables, were being prepared, and that an early settlement could be anticipated.[31] Eventually Francis agreed to all that was asked of him, although not without a lot of haggling, and kept up his payments until the outbreak of war in 1522.

Mary's state of mind at this juncture is hard to assess. Immediately after Louis' death two friars had been sent from the English court, ostensibly to commiserate with her on the loss of her husband, but in reality to pursue a party agenda. One of them, Bonaventure Langley, was the same man who had taken Catherine's condolences to Margaret in Scotland after the death of James IV, and it is natural to suppose that she was again responsible for his despatch. The circumstances were similar, and it is reasonably certain that they had not been briefed by the King or Wolsey.[32] They apparently knew about Henry's 'waterside promise' to allow her to choose her own mate the second time around, and set out to persuade her that he had no intention of keeping it. They also knew that Suffolk was on his way, and tried to persuade her that his instructions were to bring her back so that the King could renegotiate her marriage to Charles. Their mission left her unpersuaded, but in a state of considerable distress. When Suffolk arrived and discovered what had happened, he had no hesitation in blaming the Howards, whom he knew were in alliance with Catherine to attempt the resurrection of the Imperial connection and the overthrow of the continuing relationship with France which both he and Wolsey favoured.[33] Mary meanwhile had decided to take an initiative. If she remained in France, the chances of her being married to a French nobleman were very high. It is probable that she exaggerated Francis's own interest, because he would have had to divorce Claude in order to marry her, and there is no suggestion that he contemplated such a course. If, on the other hand, her brother was successful in his bid to recover her, there seemed every likelihood that he would marry her to a partner of his own choosing. His relations with Francis, although outwardly cordial, were in fact suspicious. They were too much alike in their youth and ambition to be anything other than rivals, and the Queen Dowager looked suspiciously like a hostage for Anglo-French relations. So she raised with Brandon the possibility of acting upon Henry's earlier promise before he had any chance to renege, and of marrying him secretly while still in France. It is very unlikely that this was an emotional or impulsive decision, and was probably discussed long and hard over many days.[34] Francis, at any rate, got wind of what was afoot, and in welcoming Suffolk as an envoy, declared that he was pleased to learn that he had come to marry the Queen Dowager, an intention which at that time the Duke disowned.[35] Such a marriage was an acceptable compromise as far as the French King was concerned, because it would enable him to release Mary without running the risk that she would be used against him.

5

MARY & THE DUKE OF SUFFOLK

The origins of the relationship between Mary and Charles Brandon went back some way. He certainly had an eye for a pretty girl, and she may well have been attracted by her brother's dashing friend. He had been the King's chosen jousting companion since Henry had first entered the lists in public in 1510, and was well known for his gallantry, in both senses of the word. Whether there had been any discussion of the possibility of marriage between them we do not know, but Polydore Vergil, writing many years later, thought that there had, and attributed Brandon's promotion to the dukedom of Suffolk to that consideration.

> Many people considered it very strange that Charles should be so honoured as to be made a Duke [Vergil wrote] ... the dignity was intended, as was apparent afterwards, to enable him more properly to be related to the king in marriage, this future development having already been decided upon by the King ...[1]

This is almost certainly wrong, because she was firmly betrothed to Charles of Castile at that point, and also because it implies a gift of foresight on Henry's part that he could not possibly have possessed. It may well have been that the possibility had been raised, in which case it would have been raised by the Princess, who may well have been looking for a way out of her commitment to the Prince. It would have been unthinkably presumptuous for Brandon to have broached such a topic to the King. In any case, whatever understanding they thought that they had was set aside when peace with France was on the agenda. Henry apparently dropped hints that his sister was available, and that he favoured a foreign marriage for her, the implication being that he found her existing betrothal unsatisfactory.[2] 'This coming to King Louis' ears, he sought both peace and marriage,' wrote Vergil, and he added truthfully enough that Pope Leo, who was the leader of the war alliance, was also determined upon peace, 'so there was no gainsaying it'.[3] So Mary repudiated her engagement to Charles, and was betrothed instead to Louis, a man almost old enough to be her grandfather. She was undoubtedly motivated by the thought of becoming Queen of France, but we do not know what other inducements Henry may have offered, or whether Charles Brandon featured in them. What we do know is that when the King went to the waterside in Dover to see his sister off to France, he then promised that in the event of the ailing Louis not lasting long, she would be free to choose her own partner thereafter.[4] Brandon's name does not seem to have been mentioned, but in view of the discussions which had already been held, we may presume that he could be taken for granted.

During the Duke's embassy to France in November 1514, no mention was made of this relationship, for obvious reasons. Suffolk's secret mission was to the King, and Mary was not involved in any of the negotiations. When he distinguished himself in the lists, it was in her honour, but that was because she was the Queen, and he does not seem to have worn her favour. By the time that he arrived the 'bedchamber crisis' had already been resolved by the Earl of Worcester, and there is no record of them having any private meetings. When he returned to England at the beginning of December, he reported her general well-being and happiness, but nothing more intimate. At the same time he was clear that Louis was a sick man, and although the Duke had secured his agreement to a meeting with Henry in the spring, it was by no means certain that he would last that long.[5] So anxious was Wolsey at this that he actually anticipated the news of the King's death by writing to Mary early in January, urging her not to commit herself to any further marriage if Louis should die, a letter to which she replied on the 10th, as we have seen.

> I pray you as my trust is in you for to remember me to the King my brother for such causes and business as I have to do for as now I have no other to put my trust in but the King my brother and you, and as it shall please the king my brother and his council, I would be ordered, and so I pray you my Lord to show his grace saying that the king my husband is departed to God of whose soul God pardon … I trust I have so ordered myself since that I came hither that I trust hath been to the honour of the king my brother and me since I came hither and so I trust to continue …[6]

It is a very self-possessed letter, and one which shows that she knew very well what she was about. In an exchange of letters with the King and with Wolsey, she nevertheless revealed the extent of her anxiety. Trapped in the Hotel de Cluny, she felt isolated and vulnerable, cut off from her own people. Her English servants had been dismissed after Louis' death, and replaced with French women, whom she did not trust. This action had presumably been taken by the Council, or by Louise of Savoy without Francis's knowledge, because when she retaliated by dismissing her French attendants and reinstating the English, he did not object.[7] Her surviving letters from this period present something of a problem, because they all appear to be drafts, full of rewritings and corrections. She certainly used Wolsey as an intermediary with Henry, and sent the Archbishop her thoughts, which he then put into a form which he knew would be acceptable to the King, so these must be her rough versions.[8] Henry then responded with smooth reassurances of support. On 14 January he wrote to Francis, expressing his regret for Louis' death, and congratulations upon his accession. He would, he intimated, shortly be sending a mission consisting of Brandon, Wingfield and West to sort out relations between the kingdoms in the new circumstances, and to negotiate Mary's future. Francis, whose ambitions were focussed on Italy, was keen to renew the alliance with England, but reluctant to allow Mary to depart for fear that Henry would renew her betrothal to the Archduke Charles, or find some other equally unacceptable partner for her.[9] The King may have had some such thought in mind, but Mary was at pains to remind him of his 'waterside promise', which she was now insistent that he should honour. Since it would have been inconsistent with his chivalric code to have broken his promise to a lady, Henry now faced a dilemma. He discussed the matter with the Duke of Suffolk before his departure, and he seems to have agreed that he would accept some level of commitment to her on the Duke's part; enough to persuade Francis to release her, but short of a full marriage. Indeed he extracted a promise from Suffolk that he would not marry her until after their return, perhaps intending to keep his options open in that direction.[10] Polydore Vergil's account of what happened reveals a level of misunderstanding which was generally shared in the court:

> The envoys came to Paris and explained to Francis the orders they had been given by Henry. Francis agreed with the greatest alacrity to perform all that was asked, except that it was quite clear that the departure of the girl seemed to be regarded by him with displeasure. Henry had anticipated this and ordered Charles to marry her; this was done in accordance with a decision taken before her French marriage … Francis rejoiced greatly at this since he had feared that she might be given to Charles, King of Castile. So Mary, having lost her first husband, yet returned home a wife …[11]

The French King's 'alacrity' to pay the sums demanded may be doubted, as there was considerable wrangling over this before an agreement was finally thrashed out, and Suffolk had certainly not been 'ordered … to marry her'. However an understanding of some kind had been reached, and it was not as secret as it should have been, because when Suffolk reached Paris towards the end of January he was welcomed by Francis on the grounds that he had come to marry the King's sister, an ambition which the Duke was constrained to deny. However, when he met Mary, perhaps later that same day, he found that her mind was made up. She would 'have none but me' as he confessed to the King a few days later, and was quite prepared to accept the responsibility for her own actions. She had, he alleged, besought him with floods of tears, but it is unlikely to have happened in such a fashion.[12] Mary was a champion weeper when the occasion demanded, but this was no emotional decision, let alone a 'hysterical' one as has been claimed. It was a rational course of action, designed to placate Francis and to secure her release from Cluny. Nor was it a sudden decision, as Suffolk claimed. It was earnestly discussed between them over several days, as the risks of incurring Henry's displeasure were weighed against the advantages of the French King's favour. It remains something of a mystery what had passed between Mary and Francis that persuaded her into this drastic course of action. She knew, of course, that he was proposing several French noblemen as her prospective husband, but she also knew that he would be unable to force such a choice upon her without fatally disrupting his relations with Henry VIII. He had visited her at Cluny several times both before and after his coronation, and on one of his early visits she had assured him that she was not pregnant. Louise of Savoy did not trust her assurances, but the King apparently did, and went ahead with the plans for his crowning on that understanding.[13] On a later visit, according to Mary, he made some suggestions 'not conducive to her honour', which presumably means an offer to make her his mistress. It seems that he felt he owed this to himself, and was not too disconcerted when she rebuffed his advances; indeed they may not have been very seriously intended. On 15 February, some two weeks after her commitment to Suffolk, she wrote to her brother:

Pleaseth it your grace, the French King on Tuesday night last came to visit me, and had with me many divers [discourses], among the which he demanded me whether I had made any promise of marriage in any place, assuring me upon his honour, upon the word of a prince, that in case I would be plain [with] him in that affair he would do for me therein to the best of his power, whether it were in his realm or out of the same. Whereunto I answered that I would disclose unto him the secret of my heart in humility as unto the prince of the world after your grace in which I most trust, and so declared unto him the good mind which for divers considerations I bear to my Lord of Suffolk, asking him not only [to grant] me his favour and consent thereunto, but [also] that that he would of his own hand write unto your grace and pray you to bear your like favour upon me. The which he granted me to do, and so hath done … Sir I most humbly beseech you to take this answer which I have made unto the French King in good part, the which I did only to be discharged of the extreme pain and annoyance I was in by reason of such suit as the French King made unto me not according with mine honour, the which he hath clearly left off …[14]

This is slightly less than explicit in that it does not actually confess that the marriage had taken place, still less been consummated. Somewhat alarmed at his failure to respond, she reminded him of his promise, and threatened that if he did not approve of her action, she would take herself off to 'some religious house', and thus remove herself from the dynastic equation altogether. Eventually it was left to the Duke to explain to Wolsey what had actually happened. Writing on 5 March, about a month after the event, he declared that on his arrival in Paris he had heard many things which put him and the Queen in great fear, and the queen would never let me be in rest till I had granted her to be married; and so, to be plain with you, I have married her heartily, and have lain with her in so much as I fear me but she be with child.[15]

He begged Wolsey to break this news to the King as gently as possible, lest he find out by some other route and be displeased. It seems that the Archbishop did not fully comply with this request because it was apparently after that (the letters are undated) that Henry wrote to Suffolk, treating his marriage as a hypothetical possibility, and saying that its successful consummation would depend upon the Duke's success in getting a favourable financial settlement out of Francis.[16] Since her jewels, and particularly the Mirror of Naples, were bones of fierce contention between the English and French negotiators, this was no mere rhetorical reservation. Just when the King actually found out that his consent had been taken for granted, we do not know, but 'displeased' would be an understatement of his reaction. He was very annoyed, not so much by the fact of the marriage, which can hardly have come as a surprise to him, as by the manner in which it had come about. Brandon had promised him that he would do nothing in that connection until the couple were safely back in England, and he had broken his word. It did not matter that Mary had solicited him; the responsibility was his. He was a man, and the man was always responsible for the political actions of any woman with whom he might be associated; equally important, by breaking his promise he had broken trust and betrayed the code of honour which he shared with the King.[17] Wolsey was even more disconcerted by Suffolk's confession, because to marry a blood relation of the King without explicit consent was a treasonable offence, no matter what the mitigating circumstances. He wrote condemning the Duke with the full weight of his archepiscopal authority, but at the same time offering a possible way out. Suffolk had no option; faced with the King's indignation he remitted his case 'wholly to your [grace's] discretion', agreeing in advance to do whatever might be required.[18] At about the same time Mary wrote to Henry complaining of 'her greatest discomfort sorrow and desolation' at being advertised 'of the great and high displeasure which your grace beareth unto me and my Lord of Suffolk for the marriage between us', and protested that it was only the 'great despair' brought by the two friars out of England which had persuaded her to that course.[19] Meanwhile she had smuggled out the Mirror of Naples as a peace offering to her indignant brother, and accepted whatever financial penalties he might choose to impose. In spite of his anger, Henry did not really want the Duke's head; he had too high a regard for him, and therefore proved equally amenable to Wolsey's proffered solution. On 9 March Mary signed a document assigning her whole dowry to Henry as part of a financial settlement with the King of France which was fully satisfactory to the English. Francis had come good on his offer of support, and his negotiators had given way on a whole range of topics. As Mary put it in another letter, 'The French king speaketh very kind words unto me [because] he hath a special mind to have peace with your grace before any Prince of Christendom.'[20]

The success of Suffolk's diplomacy compensated to some extent for his *faux pas* over the marriage. In addition to paying the balance of the English King's pension, as Louis had earlier agreed, Francis accepted an obligation to pay Mary £40,000 a year as her dower, and to repay the 200,000 crowns which she had brought with her in dowry. He also allowed her to take back to England all the jewels and plate which she had brought with her on her arrival in France, although not those which had been given to her subsequently. The fact that the Mirror of Napes had already been sent to England remained as a bone of contention, and nothing was said about the future of Tournai, which the French King had been keen to recover.[21] These matters being settled, it was intimated to the Duke and his wife that the King's anger was sufficiently mitigated to allow them to return to England, and they left Paris on 16 April. Before going, Mary signed receipts for 20,000 crowns in travelling expenses, 200,000 crowns for her dowry, and for the Mirror of Naples. The fact that she was required to sign a separate receipt for the latter indicates its importance as an unresolved issue. By this time Mary and Suffolk had undergone a second and more public wedding in Paris on 31 March, and Louise of Savoy noted in her journal that the Duke, 'homme de bonne condition' whom Henry had sent as ambassador to Francis, had wedded Mary, the widow of Louis XII.[22] There could now be no denying the fact of their union, and Louise, no doubt with a sense of relief, noted their departure for England just over a fortnight later. Mary, however, was still sore that she had been required to seek the King's forgiveness for an action which she believed he had sanctioned in advance. On 30 April, just before leaving Calais, she had written to her brother with some indignation, reminding him again that she had been 'contented and agreeable' to her marriage with Louis only on the condition that should she chance to outlive him 'I might with your good will freely choose and dispose myself to any other marriage at my liberty' without incurring his displeasure, 'wherunto ye condescended and granted as you well know'.

Whatever promises Suffolk had made, Mary clearly felt that the King was equally bound, and that his indignation was not conducive to his honour.[23] Whether he was moved by her reprimand or not, when the couple landed at Dover on 2 May, the King awaited them at nearby Birling House, with a great and honourable retinue, and he graciously accepted her explanation that she had been entirely responsible for what had happened in France. The Howards, who had hoped to seize the opportunity created by the King's rage to break Suffolk's special relationship with Henry, were disappointed of their prey, and constrained to feign friendship, which probably deceived no one but was necessary to the harmony of the court.[24]

Wolsey, meanwhile, was anxious to take the credit for having smoothed the ruffled feathers of his indignant master. He had played on Henry's greed, and set up a financial settlement with the Suffolks which placed them at the King's mercy for the foreseeable future. Mary was required to pay £2,000 a year for the next twelve years, or until the sum of £24,000 had been discharged, while the Duke had to forfeit the wardship of Elizabeth Lisle, and they were jointly bound in the huge recognisance of £100,000 to give up all the plate and jewels which the Queen Dowager had received.[25] The jewels were indeed surrendered, but the repayments of the debt were but slackly enforced. According to one account only £1,324 had actually been paid by 1521, which suggests that Wolsey was satisfied with having made his point, and was not anxious to pursue them.[26] These matters being settled to the King's satisfaction, the couple were then married for a third time in a formal ceremony held at Greenwich on 13 May in the presence of the King and Queen. Mary was now, in the sight of the court and of the world, the Duchess of Suffolk.

The man to whom she had committed herself had risen through the ranks of the aristocracy. His grandfather, Sir William Brandon, had been the first of his line to emerge from the obscurity of a Norfolk merchant family. He had done so in the service of John de Mowbray, Duke of Norfolk, who had died in 1476. The Duke had rewarded him with local offices, with a seat in Parliament, and with a marriage to Elizabeth Wingfield, the daughter of a more senior Mowbray servant. Before the Duke died, and presumably with his blessing, Brandon secured a place in the service of the Crown, first of Henry VI and subsequently of Edward IV.[27] After Mowbray's death, he remained in the royal service, and like most of the Duke's affinity, did not move on to serve the Howards. Like many of Edward's household retainers, he gambled on the overthrow of Richard III and his eldest son, another William, died fighting for Henry at Bosworth. Sir William himself enjoyed a trusted place in the local government of Suffolk until his death in 1491, when his second son, Sir Robert, inherited his East Anglian lands and influence.[28] Charles, who was born in 1484, was the son of that William who had died at Bosworth, but thanks to the accidents of mortality inherited virtually no lands. His uncle Robert, who was by all accounts a quarrelsome individual, was little help to him beyond giving him an introduction into Suffolk gentry society. His mother had been an heiress, but her property passed on her death to her son by a previous marriage, and Charles's attempts to recover that small proportion which should have come to him were unsuccessful. Neither in 1504 nor 1509 did he hold that £40 a year in lands which would have required him to seek the honour of knighthood. Charles owed his introduction to the court to his younger uncle, Sir Thomas, who had followed his father in the royal household. Thomas had become an Esquire of the Body by 1489, and in the 1490s had been an extremely active courtier, taking part in jousts and in the King's revels. He became Master of the Horse in 1501, and in that capacity commanded quite a lot of patronage.[29] One of the beneficiaries of this was his nephew, Charles, who attended on Prince Arthur in some unnamed capacity at his wedding, and shortly afterwards appears as a sewer in the royal household. By the time he was twenty-one, in 1505, he had become Master of the Horse to the Earl of Essex who was a prominent courtier, and played a leading part in the jousts which were organised in 1506. He was made an Esquire of the Body in 1507, and seems to have become friendly with the Prince of Wales at that point.[30] Perhaps because of this, as well as his connection with Essex, when Henry VIII established his band of spears in October 1509, with Essex as Lieutenant, Charles Brandon became a member. This in itself was of no great significance, but by that time he had become close to two of Henry's other favourites, Thomas Knyvett and Edward Howard, and the three of them featured prominently in the numerous court jousts which were organised between 1509 and 1511, usually jousting on the King's side.[31] By the time that his uncle Sir Thomas died in January 1510, Charles was well established in the King's favour in his own right, and the death of his one-time patron made no significant difference to him.

The martial ardour of this trio probably encouraged the King in his pursuit of war with France in 1512, and certainly did nothing to restrain him, but the actual development of hostilities did not correspond with the chivalric dream. At the beginning of August 1512 Brandon and Sir Henry Guildford were entrusted with the command of troops for Sir Edward Howard's attack on Brittany. However, the ship in which they were placed was unable to intervene when Sir Thomas Knyvett's *Regent* was grappled by the *Cordeliere* out of Brest. The *Cordeliere*'s magazine exploded, and Knyvett, along with most of his crew were killed.[32] He had been granted that command as a special mark of royal favour, and his death affected his companions deeply. Howard indeed vowed that he would never look the King in the face again until he had avenged him, a vow which led indirectly to his own death in action in the following year. He tried, with inadequate support, to take out the French galleys which were defending the Breton coast, and was thrust over the side and drowned.[33] Henry was deeply distressed by the loss of two of his three chosen companions, but the consequences for the survivor were wholly beneficial. In the short term he was equally distressed, acting as executor for his 'special trusty friend' and receiving the chain which had held the Lord Admiral's whistle until he had cast it away shortly before his death. However, with the departure of Howard, Charles had also lost the only man who consistently outshone him both in the court and in war, and it was natural that in consequence he should become the King's closest friend. From 1512 to 1514 he took on the distinctive role which that position implied. No one took part in more disguisings or jousts than he did, and no one was so closely matched with Henry in apparel. It is significant that both Howard and Brandon were elected to the Order of the Garter on 23 April 1513, but because of the former's continued absence at sea, he did not receive his award, and on account of his death in early May never achieved it.[34] In both April and May Brandon received important grants from the King, and set the seal upon his now unique position. It would appear that he had already secured supremacy in the lists, because Howard's failure to return to the court after Knyvett's death had left him without a serious rival. On 1 June 1512 he and Henry challenged alone together for the first time, and this was to be repeated on numerous occasions over the next two years.[35]

Charles Brandon had first entered the lists as soon as he entered the court. In 1501 he was noted as performing well in the splendid tournament of that year. At seventeen, he must have been just about the youngest participant, and thereafter he went from strength to strength. The only esquire among the six challengers at the coronation jousts in 1509, thereafter he was a regular member of the team of three or four challengers led by the King, and was always at the centre of the allegorical displays which characterised these performances.[36] So how good a jouster was he? Good enough, it would seem, to beat every opponent who came against him, except the King. Contemporary accounts need to be treated with caution, because their usual purpose was to glorify Henry, and Brandon seems not to have jousted against Sir Edward Howard, perhaps for good reason. Jousting is a sport in which the contestants need to be evenly matched, and in which it is quite possible for the skilful to fake a result. So we should probably conclude that Charles was adept enough to let the King win without sacrificing any of his credibility.[37] This appears to have happened in February 1511, when in the last two runs he failed to score, leaving Henry with a victory which was apparently hard fought, and the glory which he always sought. During celebratory jousts at Tournai in October 1513, the King and Brandon wore identical costumes, 'a remarkable thing' as one commentator noted, and a clear indication that Charles now reigned supreme as Henry's favourite.[38] Another indication of the same thing was the number of well-paid and significant offices which he collected. As early as November 1511 he had been granted the position of Marshall of the Household, jointly in survivorship with Sir John Carew, and when Carew was killed alongside Sir Thomas Knyvett in 1512, Brandon was left in sole possession. A lucrative position, this also carried with it considerable influence in Southwark, where the Marshalsea court was situated, and a principal responsibility for the King's personal security, a matter for which a good personal relationship with the monarch was essential.[39] In April 1512 he was also given a life grant of the office of Ranger of the New Forest, and took part in the King's hunts whenever his pleasure took him in that direction. This was also a position which carried a number of valuable perquisites. The following month Charles became Keeper of Wanstead in Essex, where the King also hunted, and his sister Mary was in residence from time to time, although how much advantage Brandon took of that circumstance we do not know. Then, on 6 October 1512, he was granted the prestigious office of Master of the Horse, his uncle's old position which had been held since 1510 by Sir Thomas Knyvett. This carried with it the right to appoint to all the inferior posts within the stables, but only when they fell vacant, which tended not to happen very often as these were desirable appointments.[40] Although not the most important of household positions, the Mastership carried with it special rights of access to the King, and a place close behind Henry when he rode in procession, which was frequently. The Master of the Horse was the King's esquire, and this carried particular prestige in the Low Countries because the Burgundian equivalent was a much more magnificent personage.

Brandon's prominence was reflected in May 1513 in his appointment to command an expedition against Brittany designed to revenge the death of Sir Edward Howard. Because of divided councils and administrative mismanagement the raid never actually took place, and Lord Thomas Howard, who had succeeded his brother Sir Edward as Lord Admiral, blamed Brandon. This was an unfair simplification of a very complex situation, but it led to a falling out between the two men which was to be of lasting significance.[41] Howard was, however, right in one respect; that Charles Brandon had neither the status nor the experience for such a senior command, which carried with it authority over such seasoned warriors as Sir William Sandys and Sir Maurice Berkeley. These had, admittedly, blotted their copy books during the Guienne campaign of the previous summer, and the need to redeem themselves may have made them amenable, but the fact remained that Brandon was a tyro.[42] It was partly to compensate for this fact that Henry created him Viscount Lisle on 15 May, when his appointment was announced, but his 'fire new stamp of honour' would hardly have been current during the campaign, if it had ever happened. It stood him in good stead, however, during the expedition in which he did take part: the Army Royal which Henry led in person to Picardy at the end of July. There was no question of Brandon being in overall command on this occasion, but he did lead the vanguard of the King's ward – a little over 3,000 men – and was High Marshall of the whole army, with responsibility for its discipline. His court sat thrice a week throughout the campaign, and had jurisdiction over all ranks, being particularly concerned with disputes between captains and their men. In this capacity he performed well, and the good discipline of the army was much commented upon.[43] When he commended himself to Henry's ally, Margaret of Austria, Brandon was described as the 'second man' of the army, and when Tournai was captured, Henry briefly handed it over to his friend to search and guard the city and to be responsible for law and order until Sir Edward Poynings took over as Lieutenant.[44]

By the autumn of 1513 Viscount Lisle was clearly Henry's leading courtier, yet he was living from hand to mouth because of the expensiveness of life at court. He had owed Henry VII £70 on the latter's death, and had to exploit the offices he held for all they were worth – £300 a year from his Welsh holdings, £100 a year from the Mastership of the Horse, and so on, down to £6 13s 4d as an annuity on part of his ward Elizabeth Grey's estate. Of course his proximity to the King brought him patronage, and encouraged inducements from potential suitors, even extending as far as a 'retainer' of £100 a year from the Countess of Salisbury. However, most of these gifts were unpredictable assets, and Brandon's regular income was never quite sufficient to cover his increasing commitments.[45] The fact is that he did not command a large and coherent landed inheritance, and the lands that he did hold were on insecure tenures or the result of wardships which would soon come to an end. Henry gave him 20 marks a year when he created him Viscount Lisle, but that was an insignificant sum, and for some reason the King was not generous with grants of real estate. Many were therefore surprised, and indeed shocked, when Viscount Lisle was raised to the dukedom of Suffolk on 1 February 1514. The King gave him an additional annuity of £40, but that was little enough to support his new dignity, and it may well be that the Earl of Surrey, created Duke of Norfolk at the same time, regarded him with a certain contempt. Surrey had been elevated as a reward for his victory at Flodden, and Suffolk ostensibly for his role in the King's victory in France, but there was no comparison between their resources. Norfolk was a peer of the old school, with lineage and wide estates; Suffolk was a creation of a different kind, for services to the King in his personal capacity as a friend and companion.[46] It is highly unlikely that Henry had considered repairing his friend's fortune by marrying him to his sister, whatever the popular voice may afterwards have said. His power, moreover, remained that of a courtier and confidant, very much to the fore in ceremonies, but not conspicuous for his attendance at the council. That aspect of service he was content to leave to Thomas Wolsey, who had risen spectacularly in the King's confidence as a result of his handling of the logistics in 1513. This division of responsibility suited both of them very well, and in spite of disagreements over the Tournai campaign, they apparently worked in close co-operation. This relationship was to prove very useful to both of them when Brandon was sent in embassy to France in the autumn of 1514.[47]

Meanwhile the Duke of Suffolk's matrimonial history was colourful and complicated; indeed it was not entirely clear that he was free to marry Mary when the opportunity presented itself. He had set off in this direction in 1503, when at the age of nineteen he had confessed his love for Anne Browne, the daughter of Sir Anthony Browne. Charles and Anne were betrothed before the council of his then patron the Earl of Essex, and she became pregnant. A marriage so entered into and consummated should have been binding, but within months Brandon had abandoned his bride and married Dame Margaret Mortimer, a woman twenty years his senior and well endowed with property. On 7 February 1507 he had licence to enter upon her lands, which he promptly began to sell.[48] Having apparently got what he wanted out of this relationship, he then had the marriage annulled on the grounds of consanguinity, and returned to Anne, by that time the mother of his daughter. He married her secretly early in 1508, but her family were not satisfied that he would not take advantage of this secrecy to use her as he had before, and insisted upon a public ceremony. This was held after Easter at St Michael's Cornhill in the presence of a substantial number of responsible witnesses – just to be on the safe side. Anne bore Brandon a second daughter, but died of the after-effects in the summer of 1510. Charles then entered into a contract of marriage, *per verba de futuro*, with Elizabeth, Lady Lisle, whose wardship he had been granted.[49] However, Elizabeth was only eight, and it seems unlikely that the twenty-seven-year-old Brandon intended to wait for her to grow up, so the contract between them was not binding. When the army was in Picardy in the late summer of 1513, he commenced a flirtation with no less formidable a lady than the Regent of the Netherlands, Margaret of Austria. This was taken seriously by some continental observers, who noted that he had proffered his services to her, without explaining exactly what that meant. She spent lavishly in entertaining him; they danced all night and exchanged rings in the classic mode of the courtly love ritual. On one occasion he filched a ring from her, and declined to return it, which was another courtly love device. Although she was only slightly older than Brandon, she was a tough widow and never had the slightest intention of marrying him.[50] However, their games were widely misinterpreted, much to her embarrassment, and the anger of her father, the Emperor Maximilian. Henry was forced to threaten death to anyone who spread such rumours in England, and cancelled Brandon's commission to raise troops in the Low Countries in 1514. What he was not prepared to do was to order Charles to honour his contract with Lady Lisle, in spite of having conferred the viscountcy on him in her name.[51] It may be that by early 1514 he had a different matrimonial destiny in mind for his friend.

By the time that Suffolk married Mary in February 1515, his power was great, and his influence greater still, but its base was fragile. He controlled relatively little land, and most of that was linked to Elizabeth Lisle's wardship which he had to surrender as part of his deal with the King. Nor was he in any position to create an affinity, being seriously short of *manred*. His position in Wales was strong in theory, but only in the marches did he hold any effective authority. His offices paid well, but gave him no *gravitas* in council, and his influence in government depended entirely upon his relationship with the King, and that favour was a mixed blessing. His success as a courtier had raised jealousy and enmity, and he needed good marriage to consolidate his position. That, for a variety of reasons he had managed to obtain by May 1515. Unfortunately one of Mary's last actions as Queen Dowager before she left France had been to seal an instrument transferring all her jewels and other possessions to her brother, which left her in theory penniless.[52] In practice it made her dependent on Francis for the payments from her dower lands, which for the time being he maintained in full, making her husband dependent upon her for the bulk of his income, which was not a situation conducive to his peace of mind. For a while, following their third wedding, the couple kept a relatively low profile, perhaps as a result of emotional exhaustion, as much as by conscious choice. However, Mary was twenty years old, and by nature resilient, while the Duke needed to demonstrate the extent to which he had recovered the King's favour. So before the end of the year their chief concern was to resume their normal position in the life of the court.[53] This they largely succeeded in doing, Brandon taking his accustomed place in the lists in October and November, and Mary decorating the revels as she had been wont to do before her French adventure. Henry's attitude towards his favourite was curiously ambivalent, because in spite of the severity of the financial settlement, and the very evident signs of his anger, in February 1515 he had granted him almost the whole of the de la Pole estates, and made no attempt to cancel that grant when the fact of his marriage became known.[54] In fact this meant mainly reversionary rights, because the King had already granted many of the manors for terms of lives or years, and if Brandon wanted to gain immediate access, this meant buying out the holders. This his agents had begun doing before he returned from France, borrowing heavily in the process, so that he was forced to slow down on this acquisitive process after he came back. However, establishing himself as a magnate in the place of the de la Poles became a major concern of Brandon's during the summer of 1515, and he took advantage of the fact that Henry was hunting in Suffolk in July, both to visit the court and to conduct a personal progress around East Anglia.[55] In this he was accompanied by his wife, who made something of a triumph of the tour, being met with royal honours at Butley Priory, and a receiving a huge array of presents at both Norwich and Great Yarmouth. The Duke's status was further enhanced when Nicholas West, the Bishop of Ely made him Steward of the estates of the diocese in December 1515. Suffolk deliberately set out to replace the de la Poles and by early 1516 was well on his way to success.[56] He featured regularly on royal commissions in East Anglia, and may well have felt that time spent away from the court in the autumn of 1515 had not been wasted. Whether the French Queen shared this sentiment is not known, but within a year of their return to England in

2. Alleged to be the wedding portrait of Mary and Charles Brandon, it is probably later in date. By an unknown artist.

3. Mary Tudor as a young girl. By an unknown artist.

4. Mary as Queen of France, drawn in late 1514. This is the only authentic likeness.

5. Anne Boleyn, the second Queen of Henry VIII, from a drawing by Hans Holbein. Mary was deeply suspicious of her ambitions, and those of her family.

Above: 6. Catherine Willoughby, the secon Duchess of Suffolk. A drawing by Hans Holbei *Opposite*, a rather more complete study c Catherine, also by Holbein.

7. Elizabeth of York, Henry VII's queen, and Mary's mother.

8. Mary's brother, Henry VIII, effaces his father, Henry VII; from Holbein's celebrated cartoon in the National Portrait Gallery.

9. Catherine of Aragon, Henry's first Queen, and a particular friend of Mary.

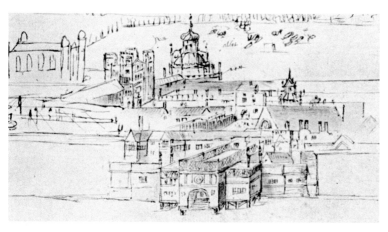

Above: 10. The English pavilion at the Field of Cloth of Gold, Henry's 1520 meeting with Francis I of France.
11. Westminster, from the panorama of London by Antony van Wyngaerde (*c*.1550). The following six pictures are all taken from the same panorama, which represents London as Mary would have known it.
Bottom: 12. Whitehall Palace.

13. London, from Westminster to the Strand.

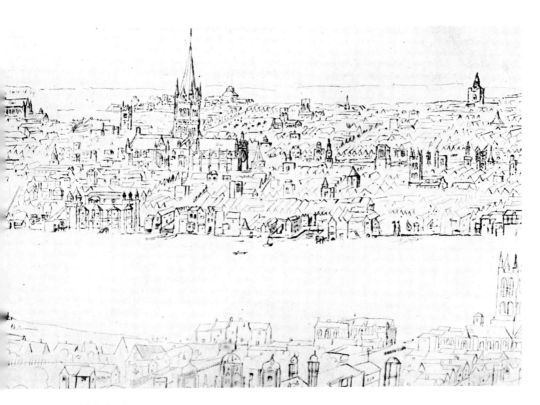

14. Old St Pauls.

15. London Bridge.

17. Cardinal Wolsey. From a drawing by
Jacques le Boucq.

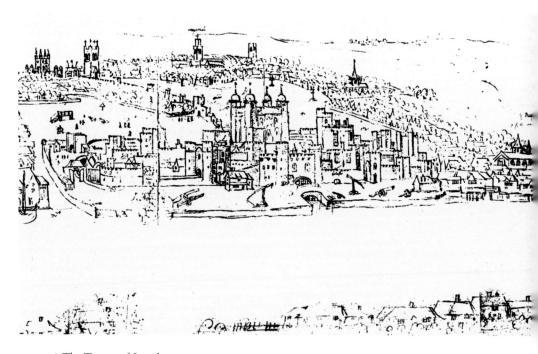

16. The Tower of London.

virtual disgrace, Mary and Brandon had settled down in London as before, and had resumed their life at court as though they had never been away. 'Henry,' as was commented at the time, 'loved a man', and no one reflected the King's glory as efficiently as the Duke of Suffolk. On 9 September 1516 Mary wrote to her 'Right dear and right entirely beloved brother' expressing her pleasure that the King was planning to visit the Duke's manor of Donnington, and that he had willed the Duke and Duchess to be there to receive him, 'much comforted that it hath pleased your grace to be pleased' to show them that especial mark of his favour. The clouds of the previous year had been thoroughly dispersed, and the sun shone again on Henry's favourite sister.[57]

6

MARY, SUFFOLK & THE KING

Suffolk's marriage to Mary brought about significant changes in his life. Any child born to the couple would have a claim to the throne, and that inevitably enhanced his status. It also carried with it the automatic right to be housed in the court, wherever that was located, including Henry's temporary palace at the Field of Cloth of Gold.[1] However, there were disadvantages in being consistently outshone by his wife. Technically, she needed his authorisation to dispose of her goods, but in their joint agreement with the King, it was her name which appeared first, and her seal was twice the size of his. When her jointure was determined by Act of Parliament, it included not only all of the de la Pole manors which had been granted to Suffolk, but also a number which he held only in reversion.[2] Between 1515 and 1519 his landed income was around £3,000 a year, but he lost the lands of the Lisle wardship by 1519, and those of Corbet and Sayle in 1522, reducing his income by about half. Of course he also enjoyed the income from his various offices, but this is hard to calculate and would not have been as much as £1,500. His financial affairs were complicated by the fact that he borrowed £12,000 from the Crown in 1515 and 1516. For this he managed to secure the backing of Italian bankers on the strength of his royal connections, and he seems to have used those connections to ensure that he was not pressed for repayment. He stalled on other creditors, and between 1513 and 1523 borrowed an additional £3,000 from the revenues of North Wales, to which he had access by virtue of his offices. From all this it appears that Suffolk was living beyond his means, or would have been if it had not been for the £4,000 a year which derived from Mary's dower lands in France, and the fact that her repayments to the King were not strictly enforced either. For these and other reasons, the Duke felt himself deeply indebted to the King of France, and consistently argued for the meeting between the monarchs which came to fruition in 1520.[3] This was all very well when relations between them were good, but when they became strained in 1516 and 1517, Suffolk became something of an embarrassment.

Mary kept her own establishment, complete with ladies and gentlewomen of the Privy Chamber, and various chamber servants to the number of about 100, which must have absorbed a fair amount of her income, but rather surprisingly only a handful of them appear to have been French. One who was was Martin Dupin, who had been an English denizen from 1512, and who appears to have been a double agent. In 1515 he was in Suffolk's service in Paris, ostensibly buying wines for Wolsey, but in 1517 he was in receipt of a French pension of 300 crowns a year for some undisclosed service, so that suspicions which focussed on the Suffolks' establishment appear to have had some justification.[4] Mary's English servants were also often in France, and William Fellowe was actually there attempting to sell off some of the 200 or more judicial offices which were at her disposal through her dower lands, when the outbreak of war forced his hasty retreat. For his part, Suffolk made no secret of his Francophilia, and cut his links with Margaret of Austria immediately after his marriage, recalling Anne, his twelve-year-old daughter, from her service. In his new circumstances he was naturally keen to draw a line under the rumours of a liaison with the Archduchess which his behaviour in 1513 had provoked.[5] Francis naturally used him as a point of contact within the English Council, and the Duke seems to have undertaken this role willingly enough. When the news of the Battle of Marignano arrived in September 1515, Henry was furious at having been so comprehensively upstaged, but Suffolk assured the messenger that he was 'as glad of the prosperity of the king my master as any man in the kingdom of France', and invited him to his house in Southwark. There he assured the envoy that the English threats of war were a sham, and in other ways undermined the King's foreign policy, to Wolsey's acute indignation.[6] He was not excluded from the Council when it was discussing anti-French policies, and was even critical of the French on some occasions, but when he began to interfere in Scottish affairs he did find himself cut out of the decision-making process. By the autumn of 1515 the pro-French Duke of Albany was established as Regent there, and Mary and Suffolk wrote to him jointly to encourage a peaceful settlement of the troubled affairs of that kingdom. This was innocuous enough, but Albany took to sending his envoys into England to visit them first, and even informed Wolsey that he should seek the truth of border disputes from the Suffolks rather than from the English officials there.[7] The Cardinal objected to this interference, and Brandon found himself excluded. His wife's role was simply ignored, although it was probably decisive in forming his attitude to Scotland, no less than to France. The fact that Mary's dower payments out of France were received erratically, even before the outbreak of war in 1522, necessitated the constant renegotiation of the Suffolks' agreement with Henry VIII. Without a regular income of £4,000 from her dower lands, there was no way in which Mary could afford the £2,000 which was due. Consequently in December 1516 the terms were modified, so that the repayments were reduced, and could cease altogether if the dower were interrupted, in spite of (or perhaps because of) the fact that none of the original payments had yet been made.[8] However, Wolsey clearly used these regular renegotiations as a means of political control, and in May 1517 he tightened up the arrangement. Mary's payments stayed at 2,000 marks (assuming her dower had arrived), but the Duke was now required to pay 500 marks towards his own debt, irrespective of what was received from France, and Mary was constrained to bequeath all her jewels and plate to the King in the event of her death, instead of to her husband. Two thousand marks' worth of jewels were handed over when the agreement was sealed, in earnest of good intentions, and the Suffolks' indebtedness was subtly increased by charging them £600 for lodgings at court, although whether the King was aware of this tariff on his hospitality remains unclear.[9]

However, all this was a burden in theory rather than practice as long as the Duke remained in favour. In July 1518 it was admitted that the indenture signed in 1517 had not been adhered to because of their 'especyall sute made unto his grace'. He was away from the court and the Council from May 1516 to February 1517, and this was widely interpreted as a sign of disfavour. However it appears not to have been the case, and probably represents an attempt by Wolsey to prevent him from interfering in the delicate state of Anglo-French relations. Henry visited the Duke at Donnington during his summer progress, and in August 1516 conferred on him (at a preferential rate) the wardships of the two sons of Sir Thomas Knyvett, who had died aboard the *Regent* four years earlier.[10] Both of these were unmistakable signs of approbation, as was the fact that Mary shared the top table with the King, the Queen and the Cardinal at a special banquet held in honour of the Emperor's ambassadors in July 1517. Mary must have understood the political significance of the occasion, but was not going to have scruples about accepting so honourable an invitation. The fact that Suffolk was active in the Council both before and after his absence, and that Henry chose to invite the Suffolks to court at Easter 1516, reinforces the view that it was Wolsey who was responsible for the Duke's absence.[11] However, by 1518 the political wind had changed direction, and the Cardinal was secretly negotiating a rapprochement with France. This made the Duke's presence in the Council desirable, and although Wolsey seems to have kept him in the dark over the progress of the negotiations, in that respect he was in no worse a condition than the majority of his colleagues. It may also have been for that reason that Wolsey apparently arranged for the Suffolks to spend the Easter of 1518 at the court, which kept the feast at Abingdon in that year. On 27 March Richard Pace, the King's secretary and the Cardinal's man of business, wrote to say that they were expected before Easter, which fell on 4 April that year, and they arrived on the 1st.[12] It suited the Cardinal very well to have the Duke at Abingdon while he got on with his business in London, and when Suffolk wrote to him on 30 April to say that their departure would have to be delayed because his wife had an ague, he was no doubt pleased enough. It may be that the Duke had earned his exclusion from the negotiations by intimating to the French ambassador that his master would be willing to surrender Tournai. If this was the case, it would have seriously undermined Wolsey's bargaining position, and would account for the coolness between them. Suffolk denied to the King that he had ever made any such suggestion, but found the Cardinal harder to persuade, and during their enforced stay at Abingdon wrote several times to plead his case.[13] He kept this bombardment up during June and July, and it was not until the end of the latter month that he was reassured that Wolsey was again his 'good lord and friend'. He had travelled from Bury St Edmunds to Enfield to confirm this news, and found the Cardinal, who had now secured his treaty with France, in a forgiving mood. He had in any case sold Tournai back to the French, so the point of his former indignation would have been rather lost. In order to confirm their renewed friendship, Wolsey negotiated a settlement between Suffolk and the Earl of Surrey, probably over the de la Pole estate, which seems to have thoroughly restored the former's peace of mind.[14]

While this was still going on, as though to demonstrate their continued closeness to the royal couple, the French Queen and the Duke of Suffolk were admitted along with the King and Queen, into the Order of the Canons Regular of St Austin in a Chapter held at Leicester on 16 June. Apart from being a sign of their accepted piety, this had no particular significance beyond obliging them from time to time to act as patrons of the order, an obligation which they do not seem to have discharged with any enthusiasm.[15] It may also have been that their admission was arranged by the King, in order to demonstrate his continued favour, because Suffolk was undoubtedly finding it difficult to maintain good relations with both Henry and Wolsey, especially when they were apart and apparently pursuing separate policies. In late July 1518 the King stayed at Wanstead, of which Suffolk was still the Keeper, and enjoyed the Duke's hospitality, a circumstance which constrained Brandon to reject an invitation from Wolsey to visit him in London. Uneasy is the position of a man who serves two masters! The renewal of Anglo-French friendship undoubtedly relieved the pressure on Suffolk's resources, because it led to the regular payment of his wife's dower 'in which restith much of her honour and profit, and mine also', as he confessed.[16] During the period of tension he had been constrained to entrust a confidential plea over this to Sir Thomas Boleyn, the ambassador in France, but such secret dealings were now needed no longer. The French Queen and the Duke were at the centre of the Anglo-French ceremonies and festivities. He reappeared as a leading councillor, and provided a lavish banquet for the whole French embassy. As far as Suffolk was concerned, it was back to the situation of 1514–15, and although Wolsey's position was now far stronger than it had been then, the King still chose to convey his instructions relating to the French hostages (or guests) to the Cardinal via the Duke of Suffolk in January 1519, a circumstance which may have taken the Lord Chancellor aback.[17]

Suffolk had not been entirely ignored by powers other than France. At a time of Anglo-French tension in 1516, when there had been rumours of war, the Emperor Maximilian had communicated with him, and seems to have envisaged him commanding an army against France. However, nothing came of the overtures, and when Maximilian's successor Charles V considered with his council the desirability of offering pensions to Englishmen, in December 1519, they agreed on Wolsey, Norfolk and Worcester, but not the Duke of Suffolk.[18] However, when relations with France cooled again in 1521, the Duke was assiduous in looking after the Imperial ambassadors, and in May 1522 was one of that select band of courtiers who accompanied Henry to meet Charles at Canterbury. On 9 June both sovereigns dined at Suffolk Place, and hunted in the park there. In that same year he secured an Imperial pension to replace the one which he had lost out of France on account of the war, and succeeded to a remarkable degree in placing his dependants on the same pension list. Half of Charles's English pensioners were Suffolk protégés, who had little to commend them except their service to the Duke.[19] By the skilful deployment of his position as a courtier, the Duke had succeeded in convincing the Emperor that his clientage was worthy of support. This was a remarkable turnaround in the space of three years, and must reflect Brandon's growing international reputation as a friend and confidant of Henry VIII. He was a man whom it was no longer safe to ignore.

His household was not particularly large, although a number of these clients were not household servants. It expanded greatly on his marriage, and his establishment became almost indistinguishable from that of his wife. Almost, but not quite, because Mary brought with her a substantial number of young ladies and gentlemen who had been nurtured in her retinue, and various kinsmen and women who had served her in France, notably Elizabeth and Anne Grey, George Brook the son of Lord Cobham, and Humphrey the bastard son of Lord Berners.[20] By 1524 Brandon had fifty-one servants who were earning more than 26s 8d each, and Mary may have had twice as many. A little earlier an old-fashioned noblemen like the Earl of Oxford would have had more than a hundred at that level, so given their status the Suffolks were not over-endowed with servants.[21] Nor did the Duke at this stage use his household to build a regional affinity. Most of his estates were in East Anglia, but there is a notable lack of East Anglian gentry among his senior servants, his two principal officers, Sir Thomas Wentworth and Sir John Burton, both coming from the West Riding of Yorkshire. As usual with a major household, there was steady throughput of servants, a number going on after a few years to other preferments, some, as in the case of Richard Long, entering the royal service, and others that of Sir Richard Lovell with whom Brandon had close connections. It was also a social beehive, with a number of Mary's young ladies finding their marriage partners among their fellows in the same establishment, or in related households such as that of John Gurney.[22] In the early 1520s Suffolk's household was costing him about £1,000 a year in wages, liveries and subsistence. This was about the same proportion of his income as that deployed by the Duke of Buckingham, but was less grand in scale because his resources were smaller. Mary paid her own servants, which was why she was in such extreme difficulties when her French revenues did not arrive, and why the accumulated debt of the couple continued to rise. The Duke's council, which should have formed the core of his household, is elusive. Sometimes it seems to have worked in London, keeping him informed about events in the capital when he was not there, but equally it appears as an executive body in Suffolk, acting as a contact between the Surveyor and the Auditor on the one hand and the local bailiffs on the other.[23] Sometimes the Duke appears to have sent an individual with executive powers rather than working through the council, and even its membership is shadowy.

In all this tangle of international commitments and domestic management, however, the most important of Brandon's tasks, and the one on which all else depended, was to keep his place by the King's side. Henry's confidence and friendship were essential to him, and in spite of the King's affection for his sister, this was an area in which he was essentially on his own. This produced occasional outbursts of acute anxiety, particularly over the renegotiations of his debt, and when he was absent from the court he feared that his place in the King's jousts might even be in jeopardy. During these absences, notably in July 1516, he occasionally wrote to Wolsey, asking him to keep the King in mind that he 'daily ... desireth to see his grace'.[24] However, it seems that his anxiety was misplaced, because when Suffolk was not at court, the King's martial feats were scaled down, and he took to challenging alone rather than finding a substitute companion in arms. The Duke's role in these entertainments certainly changed, but that was not due to any loss of favour – rather the reverse. On 29 January and 19 and 20 May 1516, Suffolk was Henry's first aid, or fellow challenger, but by 7 July 1517 he had become the leader of the answerers. The reason for this seems to have lain in the events of 20 May, when Suffolk had scored excellently and the King's performance by comparison was feeble. Henry blamed his failure on the poor quality of his adversaries, and promised never to joust again 'except it be with as good a man as himself'.[25] The only man who certainly answered that description was the Duke of Suffolk, who thereafter became the leader of the King's opponents. So the pattern changed, and Henry's team came to consist of the younger members of the Privy Chamber, such as

Sir Francis Bryan, while the Duke's aids consisted of established court nobles such as the Marquis of Dorset and the Earl of Essex. However, this was an endorsement of Suffolk's position rather than the reverse, and on 7 July the spectators were particularly impressed by the titanic battle between him and the King. Hector and Achilles were invoked as precedents, and at the end of the combat the two contestants rode out of the ring together, their struggle ended symbolically in renewed brotherhood, like that of Lancelot and Tristram.[26] This pattern continued for the jousts of the next seven years until, following an accident which could have caused Henry serious injury, the Duke vowed never to run against the King again. By that time he was forty years old, and his jousting days were in any case virtually over. Henry's confidence in his friend's ability was shown by his selection, along with the Marquis of Dorset, to be the King's chief aids in the international jousts at the Field of Cloth of Gold in 1520. Suffolk might be outshone in the disguisings and other court revels of the period, but never in the lists. His role in these revels was usually confined to dancing, although he occasionally appeared with the King disguised as 'an ancient person', to emphasise the youth of Henry's new companions. Mary also took part in these celebrations, and in other banquets and state occasions, her beauty adding lustre to the scene, but her role was essentially passive, except when she led the dancing. However, her presences at court served as a counterpoint to those of her husband, and a reminder to the King (if he ever needed it) that his favourite jouster was also his brother-in-law.

Wolsey's great diplomatic triumph, the Treaty of London of 1518, had included a clause committing Henry and Francis to a personal meeting in the summer of 1519.[27] However, the death of the Emperor Maximilian in March necessitated an election, and since both monarchs were candidates this meant the postponement of the meeting until 1520. By that time, however, the election of Charles of Castile as the Emperor Charles V had somewhat changed the political agenda. Henry, always a shade suspicious of Francis, decided that his interests might be better served by an understanding with the new Emperor, and took advantage of the latter's intended voyage from Spain to invite him to England. He duly arrived at the beginning of May, and was lavishly entertained, with hunting and banquets at which the 'beautiful Lady Mary, the King's sister, late Queen of France and now consort of the Duke of Suffolk' featured prominently.[28] The proceedings were also graced by the appearance of Queen Germaine, the widow of the King of Aragon, and now the wife of the Marquis of Brandenburg, who shared the same status as Mary, and her husband and the Duke of Suffolk feasted together. However, it was Queen Mary rather than Germaine or Catherine who led the dancing on these occasions, and her gracefulness was much commented upon. The meetings were friendly and a good understanding was reached. It was arranged that the pair would meet again following Henry's encounter with the French King, which was clearly expected to be competitive rather than amicable. Meanwhile Wolsey had been busy arranging for that encounter, and making sure that his master's honour was satisfied.[29] A site had been identified between Guisnes and Ardres, and a lavish temporary palace built to host the English events of the encounter. Workmen had been imported in large numbers and provisions of every kind laid on both for men and horses. No expense had been spared. Meanwhile the Emperor had almost outstayed his welcome, and when he eventually parted from the King at Canterbury on 30 May, he went to Sandwich to embark, and Henry, Catherine and Mary went the same day to Dover for the same purpose.[30]

There is some doubt how many attendants Mary took with her to France. The Duke of Suffolk was limited to seventy, so we may assume that the Queen took rather more, but no list survives. The royal lists include the Duke as attendant upon the King, but not the French Queen, who presumably had her own establishment. She does not feature on the Queen's 'side', which includes only the Duchess of Buckingham among fifty-seven noblewomen and gentlewomen. Catherine's total entourage numbered 1,260 persons, including servants, while Henry's totalled a magnificent 4,544, including 133 knights and noblemen. It was reckoned that 3,223 horses would be needed to mount and transport this multitude and their goods.[31] Shortly after their arrival in France it was noted that the royal family rode in a procession, with the Queen following the King, and her ladies, who numbered twenty in all, including the Queen of France attendant upon her. Her English contingent (slightly seasick) arrived at Calais on 31 May to find the French awaiting them with some impatience. They should have been at Guisnes by 1 June, but Henry pleaded for some delay, and they eventually arrived on the 7th, at which point the kings ceremoniously met, with much spurious bonhomie.[32] They then proceeded to the 'feats of arms', the challenge for which had been issued in mid-April and the site chosen a month later. This had been most carefully prepared, 'appareled, ditched, fortified and kepte of the one and of the other partie by equall number' so that neither side could claim an advantage. On the 'tree of honour' which dominated the tiltyard, the kings' shields were placed tactfully side by side, and in the jousts which followed each rode the same number of courses, and broke the same number of lances, a feat which must have required great skill on both sides.[33] The Duke of Suffolk, who had been the leading English delegate in the setting up of this tournament, did not, apparently, distinguish himself as much as had been expected. Some believed that this was out of a desire not to outshine his king, but in fact he had sustained a minor injury to one of his hands. There was also the consideration that this was an occasion which belonged to his wife, who was borne in state to the tiltyard on 11 June in a litter of cloth of gold, emblazoned with monograms of L and M, supported by Louis' emblem of the porcupine. The French welcomed their own Reine Blanche, a genuine French Englishwoman, to be preferred to Henry's Spanish wife, and so much more beautiful than their own Queen Claude, a sad little creature by comparison,[34] although magnificently attired. More imposing on the French side was the Queen Mother, Louise of Savoy, who was supported by an 'infinite number of ladies' all clad in crimson velvet and cloth of gold. There was clearly an unofficial beauty competition between the ladies, because Mary was similarly supported, and this was taken as seriously as the martial emulation of the gentlemen by the spectators. The Italians, who may not have been impartial observers, awarded the palm to the French, but Mary was always excepted from this generalisation. She was beyond comparison the most lovely lady on view.[35] Catherine might win admiration for her exotic Spanish headdress, because a fashion show was all part of the fun, but because there was no distinctive English style, the French again carried off the palm, and Mary in cloth of gold was again the exception.

On Saturday 16 June Francis went to Guisnes to be entertained to dinner by Catherine, and on the 17th Henry returned the compliment, going to Ardres to the hospitality of Queen Claude. Beyond the fact that Francis was accompanied by his mother, and was clad in cloth of gold, we do not know much about his advent, but at dinner he sat opposite the Queen at a table which was shared by Cardinal Wolsey and Mary, the French Queen.[36] The company was entertained by musicians drawn from the King's Musik and the Chapel Royal, although it is doubtful whether Francis (who was tone deaf) was as appreciative as he should have been. This entertainment was not held at Guisnes Castle, which was too small, but at the King's temporary palace just outside the town, and was a sumptuous occasion, several banquets proceeding simultaneously. The great hall was occupied by tables hosting some 130 ladies, waited on by 20 gentlemen, a custom which seems to have been peculiar to the English. Elsewhere 200 gentlemen were feasted, while in yet another room were entertained those French nobles who had accompanied their king – the Admiral, the Duke of Bourbon and others.[37] When Henry went to dine with Claude, he was accompanied by his sister, her husband, and by a party of masquers, nineteen gentlemen in elaborate disguises. It was apparently intended that the King should dine alone, as an especial mark of honour, but it is not clear that he did so, since he summoned several French nobles to keep him company. The Queen, and the Duke and Duchess of Suffolk meanwhile dined at a separate table, both women, it was noted, wearing the most sumptuous pearls. Presumably the subject of the Mirror of Naples was not raised![38] Other banquets were held elsewhere for the respective retinues, and afterwards there was dancing, led by Mary as the principal female guest, and also, probably, the most accomplished performer. The King then led his gentlemen in a masque of youth and age to entertain his hosts, which was followed by more dancing and the company returned to Guisnes still in their masquing apparel, with their minstrels playing them through the streets. It is not known how Henry performed in the dances, but if his reputation is anything to go by, it would have been boisterously. After a mass of peace, at which Wolsey preached, and an exchange of costly presents, on 25 June the English withdrew to Calais, most of their overlarge retinues were disbanded, and the King's temporary palace was demolished.[39] Henry waited at Calais until 10 July, and then went to his second scheduled meeting with the Emperor at Gravelines. In spite of the expressions of goodwill, nothing had transpired at the Field of Cloth of Gold which had changed his mind about the desirability of a deal with Charles. In fact the competitive edge which he had been constrained to maintain had probably reinforced his desire for an understanding with this unassuming but tough young man.

There had been some serious political discussion at the Anglo-French meeting, conducted mostly by Wolsey with Francis's council, which had resulted in the confirmation of the existing treaties between the countries, and an agreement that the King's daughter Mary, then aged five, should in due course marry the newly born dauphin, Francis, an understanding which sealed a friendship, but nothing more.[40] Henry, in other words had been faithful to the undertakings which he had made at the Treaty of London. Nor was he to break that faith in the discussions which now ensued. This time he realised that Charles would be accompanied by his aunt, Margaret of Austria, and decided to take his sister with him. That he chose Mary rather than Catherine for this role is curious, because Charles was equally his wife's nephew, while the Duchess of Suffolk could command no blood tie at all. It may have been that what he really wanted was the companionship of his friend, Charles Brandon, and that Mary was invited as an 'accompanying person', but it does not look that way.[41] What happened was that she met for the first time that 'dear aunt' with whom she had corresponded as Princess of Castile, and the man who had almost become her first husband. It must have been a curious meeting, but we know nothing very much about it. Henry stayed in Gravelines barely forty-eight hours, time for some serious talking, but not much time for entertainment; nor is there any record of the ladies putting on a show, as might have been expected with Mary on the scene. On 12 July he returned to Calais, accompanied by the Emperor and his aunt. This time an opportunity was found for at least one banquet, held in the newly built hall of the palace, but again, apart from diplomatic discussions we do not know what transpired. Since Catherine was in Calais at the time, presumably Mary faded into the background. There was no treaty as a result of these meetings, but a good working relationship had been established which was to bear fruit in the following year. Meanwhile King Henry was ostensibly on good terms with both his powerful neighbours, a situation which was not likely to endure in face of the fact that Francis and Charles were already squaring up to each other in Italy, and that the Emperor's territories virtually surrounded France.[42] The Gravelines and Calais meetings had, however, made it more likely that Henry would side with Charles, a situation which the Francophile Duke and Duchess of Suffolk can only have regarded with trepidation.

Mary was the better educated of the two, and may well have been the more intelligent. While the Duke maintained a pro-French stand in the Council, when he bothered to attend, his wife was a channel for French cultural influences. She dressed in the French fashion, and patronised French artists and scholars, notably 'Master Ambrose', who was a painter in the service of Cardinal Duprat. Ambrose produced some of the finest work ever seen in England, and that probably stimulated the King to patronise Lucas Horenbout and Hans Holbein, not wishing to be outshone by his sister's protégé.[43] The gardens at Suffolk Place in Southwark and at Westhorpe were laid out in the French fashion under Mary's influence and the houses were among the best decorated of any in England. Such a style was not always popular, and it should be remembered that it was for their 'French touches' that the King's minions were disciplined in 1519, a move which used to be attributed to Wolsey, but is now thought to have been the work of the whole Council.[44] There were certainly many councillors, including the Duke of Norfolk, who were opposed to Wolsey's pacific policy with regard to France, and who welcomed the King's decision to ally with the Emperor which was negotiated in August 1521. The Cardinal was entrusted with the negotiation, not because he sympathised with the intention but simply because he was by far the most experienced international diplomat that England possessed, and because he would always do the King's bidding once that had been made clear to him. One of the features of this agreement was that Charles agreed to marry the King's five-year-old daughter, who was thus transferred from the Dauphin to the Emperor. In view of the age difference between them, it is unlikely that Charles took this commitment very seriously, although Henry did (or pretended to).[45] The idea of the Treaty of Bruges was the Emperor's, but Henry accepted it and Wolsey had no option. At first its true purpose was disguised under a screen of mediation, but this was abandoned when Charles paid another visit to England in May 1522. Again there were lavish entertainments and banquets, and when he reached London on 6 June, he was received by the King and it was noted that places of honour were reserved for the Duke of Suffolk and Marquis of Brandenburg, both of whom were the husbands of Queen Dowagers. Mary played her usual part in the courtly entertainments which accompanied the visit, and her namesake the princess danced, although Charles's entourage does not seem to have included any women on this occasion. The Emperor stayed for just over a month, and by the time that he left Henry had committed himself to war with France, a commitment which was to be fulfilled in the following year because it was already too late for a campaign of sufficient scale to be prepared during that season.[46] Wolsey, who had maintained the peace against the King's intermittent bellicosity for eight years, had at last been overpowered by the logic of events, and the Duke of Suffolk found himself committed to a leading military role against his old friends. Mary faced the suspension of her dower payments, and must have been profoundly relieved by the let-out clause in her agreement with the King, because there was no way in which she could have maintained her repayments in the absence of her principal source of revenue. It would be difficult enough to manage her regular expenditure, and further indebtedness loomed.

It was June 1523 before Henry was sufficiently convinced by the Duke of Bourbon's threatened rebellion against Francis

I to commit an army to the field, and the end of July before a fresh treaty was signed between the King, the Emperor and the Duke for a joint attack.[47] Despite his poverty and the lateness of the season, it was therefore the end of August when Henry launched 10,000 men, commanded by the Duke of Suffolk from Calais, into Normandy. At first the strategy was to capture Boulogne, but by the middle of September Wolsey had changed his mind, and began to urge upon the King a direct attack on Paris. This was because Bourbon had convinced him of the feasibility of a co-ordinated assault, involving himself, Suffolk and the Emperor, which would settle the issue at a single blow, rather than the 'dribbling war' which had hitherto been envisaged.[48] Eventually Wolsey convinced Henry, and on 26 September the siege of Boulogne was called off, and Suffolk was ordered to lead his men direct to Paris. At first all went well, and they advanced 75 miles in three weeks, encountering only light resistance. The King was enthusiastic, and started to organise reinforcements to keep the campaign going through the winter. Margaret of Austria was pleased because her southern borders were protected while she annexed Friesland. And then things started to go wrong. A Spanish force had indeed crossed the Pyrenees, but were so demoralised that the French had no difficulty in containing them. The Imperial thrust from the east did not materialise at all, and Bourbon's rebellion collapsed in a matter of days.[49] As a result Paris was strengthened against any possible attack, and Suffolk was isolated and exposed. Margaret was unable to provide either money or the horsemen which had been promised, and the Burgundian forces under van Buren, upon whom the Duke had been heavily dependent for strategic advice, began to melt away. Suffolk was left with no option but to retreat, and a spell of freezing cold weather in November completed his misery. With his men dying of disease and frostbite, his disciplinary system, which up until then had functioned well, broke down, and it was a disorganised rabble that arrived back at the Channel ports in early December.[50] Henry was mortified by this news, and would not at first accept it, until confirmatory detail persuaded him of its truth. Suffolk had done his best in impossible circumstances, and in the wake of Margaret's failure to support him had declined to place garrisons in her border fortresses to protect her against French reprisals. Until the November frosts ruined his control, he had been a wise and responsible commander, and the King did not blame him for the failure. Generous rewards would not have been appropriate, but the Duke emerged from his French adventure with his reputation for loyalty and generalship undiminished, and his martial enthusiasm undimmed.[51]

This last was important, because Charles V and Margaret were keen for Henry to try again, and looked to Brandon to lead any such attack. However, English councils were divided, and neither the Emperor nor his niece had the money to pay for such a expedition. Henry wavered. Early in 1524 he was bellicose, talking of leading an army to France in person, and of enforcing his claim to the French throne, but by the spring as the financial realities began to become apparent, his ardour cooled. By the summer Wolsey was conducting secret peace negotiations with emissaries of Louise of Savoy, and welcoming overtures from Clement VII. He must have done this with Henry's knowledge, but by the late summer the King was blowing hot again. In August he was planning another army of 9,000 foot and 1,500 horse, which Suffolk was to command, and the Duke set about making preparations.[52] He chose councillors and captains, and discussed arrangements for supplies and the recruitment of mercenaries. All this came to nothing, again because the money was simply not available, and there are signs that the Duke and Duchess of Suffolk were moving in different directions. Desperate to recover her dower revenues, she was supporting the peace initiative, and there were rumours of lavish gifts to induce her to intervene with her brother. If she did so, her intercessions were of no lasting effect. The Duke, on the other hand, was an Imperial pensioner, and his payments were up to date, so he had less to lose by continuing the war, and more to gain by shadowing the King as he changed his mind. His appearances at the Council in 1524 and 1525 were erratic, but on the whole his interests lay in continuing the conflict, and that was what his continental friends in the Imperial camp expected.[53] At the beginning of 1525 Henry had virtually given up; then came the news of the Battle of Pavia. On 14 February Francis's army had been destroyed, and the King himself captured. His kingdom now appeared to be open to attack as never before, and Henry's enthusiasm for forceful intervention was immediately revived. 'Now is the time,' he said to an embassy from the Low Countries, 'for the Emperor and myself to devise the means of getting full satisfaction from France. Not an hour is to be lost.'[54] The Great Enterprise was to be revived. Unfortunately, Charles was unmoved. He had his own agenda for exploiting his victory, and replied that if Henry wanted a piece of France, he was welcome to conquer it for himself. This, it soon transpired, was beyond the King's means. Wolsey had succeeded in getting a very grudging subsidy out of Parliament in 1523, but that was nowhere near enough to cover the costs of a large military expedition, and an attempt at a new exaction, called the Amicable Grant, in 1525 failed completely.[55] Disappointed by the Emperor's response, and frustrated of his purpose by lack of means, the King veered round again and accepted Wolsey's proposal to resurrect the peace negotiations of the previous year. In the present circumstances, any such initiative was bound to be welcomed by Louise of Savoy, acting as regent during her son's captivity. John Joachim, her envoy of the previous year, returned to London in June, and on 30 August a solemn treaty was signed at the More, Wolsey's residence in Hertfordshire.[56] The Cardinal's policy at this juncture was complicated, but seems to have been aimed at restoring a balance of power between France and the Empire, which meant putting together an anti-Imperial alliance. The papacy and several Italian states were involved in this plan, which eventually took shape in the form of the League of Cognac in 1526. This involved taking advantage of Henry's disillusionment with the Emperor, and hopefully restoring him to the kind of mediating position which he had enjoyed in 1518. Such a bait was necessary because by the terms of the Treaty of the More, France had ceded no territory to England, and that had been one of Henry's declared war aims. The King's honour required significant concessions, and Louise agreed to restore his pension, originally conceded by Louis XII in 1514, together with the payment of Mary's dower. On 22 October Lorenzo Orio, a Venetian envoy in London, reported that his colleague Giovanni Giaochino had gone to Calais to fetch the 50,000 ducats which were due on the pension, together with 10,000 'for Madame Mary, the King's sister, Queen Dowager of France', to whom also were restored her dower lands. The latter were farmed to Giovanni, in an arrangement which had still to be confirmed, for 29,000 ducats a year. If this worked, and there is good reason to suppose that it did, this would have given Mary an income of almost £10,000 a year.[57] Even with the necessary deductions, this would have made her one of the wealthiest peers in England, significantly richer than her husband, whose debt repayments she was now in a position to assist. It is not surprising that Suffolk, for all his military ambitions, should have been an enthusiastic supporter of the Treaty of the More.

7

THE DUCHESS & HER CHILDREN

Despite the rumours of her pregnancy, and the fears of the Duke in that respect, it was 11 March 1516 before Mary gave birth to her first child.[1] This suggests conception in June or July of 1515, well after their final marriage, and given the passion of their early relationship, indicates that she may have had some contraceptive knowledge, which no well-brought-up young lady was supposed to possess. The birth put her in good company, because her sister Margaret, the Dowager Queen of Scots and now the wife of Archibald, Earl of Angus, although estranged from her husband and a fugitive in England, had been delivered at Harbottle Castle in Northumberland on 8 October 1515; and Queen Catherine, after years of stillbirths and cot deaths, had at last produced a healthy infant on 16 February.[2] Mary had the advantage, however, because whereas both Margaret and Catherine had borne daughters, the Duchess of Suffolk had borne a son, who, given the fact that Henry had no male heir, might one day stand in the succession to the throne. The birth took place, not at Suffolk Place, but in a house belonging to Cardinal Wolsey just outside Temple Bar, called Bath Place, which suggests that labour may have come upon her unexpectedly. She and the Duke were understandably elated. Mary had now justified her existence in the most traditional fashion, and he was able for the time being to forget the mounting burden of debt which would one day have to be faced.

The child was christened Henry, after the King, and the fact that he was pleased to accept that indicated another stage in the reconciliation between brother and sister. The ceremony was performed by John Fisher, Bishop of Rochester, assisted by Thomas Ruthall of Durham, and the King and Cardinal Wolsey stood as godfathers. Catherine, the Dowager Countess of Devon, and a daughter of Edward IV, was godmother, completing the royal credentials of this most welcome addition to the family.[3] The christening took place in the hall at Suffolk Place, with all the splendour of a state occasion, and the Duke was immensely gratified by this unmistakable sign of his rehabilitation. The font was specially warmed for the occasion, and torches lit up the wall hangings with their motif of red and white Tudor roses. The only absentee from this splendid occasion was Mary herself, who had not yet been churched and who sat in the nursery to receive her baby and his presents, together with the congratulations which were appropriate. When the ceremony was over, the procession moved from the hall to the nursery along a specially fenced and gravelled path, with various members of the Suffolk household carrying the basin, chrisom and other impedimenta. Lady Anne Grey, suitably attended, bore the infant himself, and Sir Humphrey Banaster, Mary's vice-chamberlain, his train. Spices and wine were then served by the Duke of Norfolk and other attendant peers, and the sponsor's gifts were presented. The King gave a salt cellar and a cup of solid gold, and Lady

Catherine two silver gilt pots, which were none the less welcome for not being of the slightest interest to the young prince, who presumably slept soundly through this part of the proceedings.[4]

The Duke could ill afford the expense of a London season, but Mary had her own resources, and in any case he could hardly deny her the pleasure of a reunion with her sister, who was due to visit the court at the end of April. They had not met since 1503, when they had both been children, and their meeting was expected to be the cause of much celebration. In fact they might have had difficulty in recognising each other, because although Mary was still exceptionally beautiful, thirteen years and several pregnancies had coarsened Margaret, who had never matched her sister for looks, and now retained little of her youth beyond her passionate nature. She was vain, and inconsiderate of others, with a fierce temper – more like her brother, in fact. Her vanity took the form of an extraordinary fondness for fine apparel, and Henry was told that the dresses which he had sent as a present to Northumberland after the birth of her daughter had done her health more good than all the medical attention which she had received.[5] Altogether she had collected more than forty fine gowns for her visit to the court, which she was eagerly anticipating. Margaret travelled south in easy stages during April 1516, spending Ascension (1 May) with the Duke and Duchess of Norfolk at Enfield, and reaching the capital the following day. Henry rode out as far as Tottenham to meet her and escorted her to the temporary lodgings which had been provided at Baynard's Castle. Her reception began with a state dinner, hosted by William Warham at Lambeth, and was followed by a succession of entertainments provided by the King either at Westminster or Greenwich.[6] Both Mary and Catherine were pleased to see her, and they had thirteen years of gossip to catch up on, to say nothing of their babies which must have formed a basis of common interest. Given her estrangement from her husband, and the complex political situation in Scotland, neither the King nor Wolsey expected Margaret's present marriage to survive, and no sooner had she arrived in London than the latter was hinting that she might be available on the international marriage market. He even went so far as to suggest to the Imperial ambassador the possibility of a match with the Emperor Maximilian, who conveniently happened to be a widower.[7] The Queen Mother of Scotland was not consulted about these proposals, which remained just that. She was concerned to gain her brother's support to re-establish her position in Scotland, and would not have been interested in any alternative partner. Wolsey's suggestion was in fact more to do with his desire to secure control of the Council than with any destiny for the Queen of Scots. He was concerned at this stage to balance England's relations with the Emperor against those with France, and was concentrating on persuading the King of the wisdom of this course. He therefore did not want men with strong views, like the Duke of Suffolk, confusing the issue in Council.[8]

Suffolk was not out of favour with the King. He had challenged with him at the jousts held at court on 19 and 20 May, and distinguished himself as usual. Altogether there were thirty-five contestants at this celebration, all gorgeously dressed, and on the second day Henry and the Duke ran at all comers, 'which was a pleasant sight to see'. Margaret, Mary and Catherine presided together and Catherine presented the prizes. However, Wolsey's desire to have a clear run at the Council, together with his own straitened circumstances, dictated that Suffolk found it prudent to withdraw to his estates after the tournament, and he remained away for the rest of the year. As we have seen, Henry visited them at Donnington in the course of his summer progress, and conferred various other marks of favour on the Duke, but he did not summon them back to court. He also seems to have ignored Mary's fulsome letters, in which she expressed her devotion to him and his interests. 'I account myself as much bounden,' she wrote,

> unto your grace as ever sister was to brother, and according thereunto I shall to the best of my power during my life endeavour myself as far as in me shall be possible to do the thing which shall stand with your pleasure.[9]

For the time being his pleasure was that they should remain in the country caring for their infant son, but that was probably more out of consideration for the Duke's finances than out of any reluctance to see him. Before the end of the year he had been chosen to lead a possible expedition against France, and ironically enough, was being accused with Wolsey of exercising undue influence on the King, 'whether by necromancy, witchcraft or policy no man knoweth'.[10] By the end of 1516 Suffolk's personal debt to the King stood at more than £12,000, but at about that time he was given an extension, and the terms were favourably renegotiated as we have seen in the spring of 1517. Meanwhile Mary's much larger debt stood respited until her French revenues were resumed. If this was being out of favour, then the Suffolks could clearly have done with more of it. The Duke and Duchess were never unwelcome at court, and their failure to appear had more to do with the need for economy than any coldness on Henry's part. It was probably due to subtle changes in the Cardinal's foreign policy that he reappeared at Council meetings in February 1517. Wolsey was clearly confident that he could stall their debt indefinitely if the need arose, and in effect did so later in the year.

In the spring of 1517 Catherine made a pilgrimage to the shrine of Our Lady at Walsingham, and the Suffolks, who were in Norfolk at the time, accompanied her, entertaining her on the return journey. So generous was their hospitality that the Queen felt bound to return it in the following month. However, during Catherine's brief stay with them occurred an incident which Brandon feared might well ruin his credit with the King. Ann Jerningham, an attendant of the Queen's, who must have been appealed to by one or other of the parties, brokered a betrothal between John Berkeley, one of Suffolk's wards, and Lady Anne Grey, of Mary's Privy Chamber. This was a technical offence without the King's consent, and the Duke was properly alarmed. He wrote hastily to Wolsey, 'I had lever have spent a thousand pounds than any such pageant should have been within the Queen's house and mine.' He disclaimed all responsibility, and the Cardinal succeeded in nipping the engagement in the bud, which seems to indicate that there had been no personal falling out with Wolsey during the previous year, or at least that it had been repaired by April 1517.[11] For the rest of that year, Charles and Mary divided their time between the country and the court. Mary was highly decorative, and it was at about this time that she attracted the compliment from Guillaume de Bonnivet that she was the 'rose of Christendom' and should have remained in France to be admired.[12] Brandon meanwhile resumed his role in the jousts and the revels as though he had never been away. At the end of April they visited the court, which had removed to Richmond on account of the plague, a regular migration because of Henry's intense fear of the disease. While they were there the Evil May Day riots erupted in the city, spreading fear and confusion among the foreign community. This demonstration of xenophobic fury attracted swift retribution, and a dozen of the chief offenders were quickly tried and condemned. The story then runs that it was the three queens, acting together, who interceded for them with the result that only one offender was executed.[13] This may have been so, because they were all within reach at the time, and Henry was susceptible to the pleas of women, especially as two of them (Catherine and Mary) were pregnant at the time, and the King was hoping desperately for a male heir. He might well have felt that mercy would be pleasing to God. It was later when Henry pardoned the 400 delinquents on the intercession of Cardinal Wolsey, and there is no mention of Catherine or Mary being present, in spite of the legend which attaches to that occasion. 'Then were all the gallows within the city taken down, and many a good prayer said for the king,' as one chronicler observed. The fact that many gallows had been necessary indicates that far more than the original victim had been hanged. We do not know the actual number, but it seems to have been around forty or fifty.[14]

By the time that this happened, Margaret had in any case departed. She left on 18 May to rejoin her husband, who by that time had decided to cast in his lot with the Duke of Albany. Albany was no friend to England, and Henry had anticipated this, but found it more expedient (and cheaper) to let her go. She had been entertained for over a year at a cost exceeding £2,000, and left loaded with presents to resume her frugal lifestyle. In return for these gifts the King had extracted from her a promise that she would not become involved in the current government of Scotland. However, Margaret was temperamentally incapable of adhering to such a commitment, and within a few months was deeply mired in intrigue, with the result that she was just as unhappy as she had been before her flight into England. 'I had liever be dead than live my life in Scotland,' she wrote to Lord Dacre, but Henry did not take the hint, broad though it was.[15] She was eventually divorced from Angus, much to the King's disgust, and found refuge with Henry Stewart, Lord Methven, but she did not return to England and Mary never saw her sister again. That may have been no hardship to the French Queen, as in spite of the rejoicings which accompanied their reunion, there is no sign that they were particularly fond of each other. Henry certainly seems to have found her difficult, both politically and personally; and that reinforced his affection for his younger sister, so Margaret's visit may well have been indirectly beneficial to the Suffolks.

Meanwhile Mary had given birth to her second child. Burgundian ambassadors had visited the court in July 1517, had signed a treaty of friendship in general terms, and had been lavishly entertained. Mary had appeared at these festivities in spite of her advanced state of pregnancy, but the culmination was again the jousts, which were held on the morrow of St Peter's Day, 2 August. These were held in front of a large crowd of spectators, which one commentator estimated at 50,000 (a huge exaggeration) in a specially walled tiltyard which had been built for the occasion.[16] The objective, as always, was to glorify the King, and he was only with difficulty persuaded to limit himself to a single antagonist, who was of course the Duke of Suffolk.

They ran eight courses, to the great delight (we are told) of the spectators and the contest lasted four hours, at the end of which time Henry did a spectacular dismount for the benefit of Queen Catherine and her attendant ladies. By that time Mary had been compelled to withdraw owing to the imminence of her time and, apparently neglecting the usual custom of confinement, had set out on a pilgrimage to Walsingham, presumably to pray for a safe delivery. While she was on her way, labour again came upon her unawares, so while her husband was doing his duty at the court, and keeping the King amused, Mary was taking refuge in the house of an old friend, Bishop West of Ely, at Hatfield, where, early in the morning of 16 July, she was safely delivered of a daughter, who was named Frances after the saint of the day.[17] The christening, which must have been hastily prepared, took place in the local parish church two days later, in the presence of about eighty people. The godmothers, who must have been arranged in advance, were Queen Catherine and her daughter, the infant Princess Mary. The latter, who was only just over a year old, was probably recruited at the last minute when it was clear that the child was female. Because of this, and because of the shortness of the notice, neither was present in person. The Queen was represented by Lady Boleyn, who may have been Elizabeth, the wife of Sir Thomas, or possibly Anne, the wife of Sir Edward, who was a favourite of Catherine's. The Princess was represented by Elizabeth Grey, who as a member of Mary's household would have been present anyway. The godfather was the Abbot of St Albans, who would have been the nearest senior clergyman available.[18] Altogether the christening was a low-key affair, by comparison with the pomp which had attended that of the Lord Henry, but then Frances was not thought to be dynastically significant. How long it was before the Duke saw his infant daughter is not clear, but presumably he made haste to see his wife as soon as his tour of duty at the court was completed, about the end of the first week of August. By the end of August they had retired to Westhope, which by good fortune had escaped the plague, and there they appear to have spent the winter in comparative peace.

Mary bore Brandon two more children: Eleanor, who was born some time in 1519, and a second Henry, born in 1522.[19] Nothing is known of the circumstances of these births, nor of the christenings which followed. Eleanor is supposed to have been named as a compliment to the Emperor, whose sister bore that name, in which case the Imperial ambassador may well have stood godfather, but no record says so. Henry was a replacement for their firstborn, who had died in that same year at the age of six, but so little is known about him that the standard biography of Mary ignores him altogether, treating that Henry Brandon who was created Earl of Lincoln in 1525 as the child who had been born in 1516.[20] In view of the fuss which had been made over the original, it may well be that the King and the Cardinal again stood as godfathers, but no record of his christening appears to have survived. Nor do we know anything about the upbringing of these children, who presumably grew up in the Brandon household alongside their elder half-sisters, Anne and Mary, Charles's children by Anne Browne. Frances had a nurse called Anne Kyng, but nothing is known about her. The young Earl of Lincoln was later taught by Peter Valens, a friend of John Palsgrave, who had been Mary's tutor, but that arrangement would not have begun until about 1528, and we do not know whether any of his sisters shared his lessons.[21] It is more likely that they were taught their letters rather earlier by one of the chaplains on the Duke's staff. Education was not Brandon's strong point, and their mother (or stepmother) would have supervised the upbringing of the girls, all of whom grew up literate, but with a limited command of French and no other language as far as we are aware. When the time came, the Duke found honourable marriages for all his daughters. Anne was married in 1525, at the age of nineteen, to Edward Grey, Lord Powis, who had been a ward of the Crown and whose marriage Suffolk had purchased for £1,000 sometime in 1517. His revenues were given in his livery indenture as £409 a year, which would have been adequate for a minor peer without courtly ambitions.[22] Mary was married in late 1527 or early 1528 at the age of about eighteen to Thomas Stanley, Lord Mounteagle, over whose wardship there had been a good deal of skirmishing. He was the son of Edward Stanley, Lord Mounteagle, who had died in 1523, and his lands were the subject of a dispute between his father's estate officers and Lord Darcy, who had purchased his wardship. Perhaps uncertain of the outcome, Darcy had then sold Thomas's marriage (over which he had undoubted control) to Suffolk for an undisclosed sum. Thomas obtained livery of his father's lands, to the value of £605, in 1529, and by then Mary had borne him a son, but the Duke was to have endless trouble with his son-in-law.[23] In September 1529 one of Mounteagle's servants wrote to Thomas Cromwell, who was still in Wolsey's service at that point, asking him to speak to Suffolk about the bad influence which one of the young lord's intimates was having upon him. Presumably the Duke was expected to play the heavy father, but the outcome is unknown. Thomas seems to have acquired spendthrift habits, although whether that was the cause of the anxiety at this time we do not know. By 1533 he was compelled to intervene in Lord Mounteagle's financial affairs, because the latter's debts had risen to £1,450, and the Duke was forced to bail him out.[24]

These young ladies had been simply the daughters of a senior peer, but his daughters by the French Queen were a different proposition, because they carried the Tudor bloodline and might confer on their offspring a claim to the throne. This meant that it was desirable to secure a papal confirmation of his marriage to Mary, which had not been thought necessary at the time. This was negotiated by Sir Gregory Casales, the English agent in Rome, who no doubt welcomed it as a relief from the King's own matrimonial tangle. The bull was issued in May 1528, and although vague about the birthdates of Brandon's existing daughters, was quite unequivocal on the main point. The Duke and Duchess were lawfully married.[25] In August 1529 Humphrey Wingfield, acting on the Duke's behalf, presented it to Bishop Nix of Norwich for local confirmation. The Duke of Norfolk may have been unpersuaded by this show of ecclesiastical force, because in 1530 he turned down Frances, then aged thirteen, as a bride for his son Henry, Earl of Surrey, aged about fourteen, on the ground that her dowry was not big enough.[26] Fortunately an alternative soon became available, because Thomas, Marquis of Dorset, died in October 1530, leaving his son Henry under age. The Earl of Arundel bid for his wardship, and proposed a marriage alliance with his own daughter. However Henry refused the alliance, and Arundel withdrew his bid. Suffolk then secured the approval both of the King and of the Dowager Marchioness, and purchased the wardship himself. This time the young Marquis was amenable, and the couple were married in 1531.[27] This was not the end of the matter as far as the Duke was concerned, because he found himself forced to support the young couple at court until the Marquis attained his majority in 1538. Only the younger, Eleanor, was married without financial complications, because there the initiative came from the other side. As early as 1530 (when she was eleven) the Earl of Cumberland had bid successfully for the hand of the King's niece for his son Henry. The arrangement was deferred, pending the King's pleasure, but he confirmed it before Easter 1535, and the marriage was celebrated in the King's presence in June.[28]

The marriage of his son, Henry, Earl of Lincoln, was another source of financial entanglement. A suitable heiress had become available with the death of Lord Willoughby de Eresby in October 1526. Suffolk had known the widowed baroness since, as Maria de Salinas, she had stood as godmother to his daughter Mary in 1510, and had been a feofee to the use of her husband, herself and her heirs in 1518. His bid for the wardship was presumably welcomed by Lady Willoughby, but resulted in a settlement of the estate which gave Brandon only a £40 pension to look after the heir. He was compelled to mortgage some of his Oxfordshire lands to meet a payment of 4,000 marks for this privilege, and secured a grant of the wardship in February 1529.[29] Before that grant, however, Catherine's inheritance appears to have been divided between the Crown, Lady Willoughby, and Sir Christopher, the late baron's brother. The latter was aggrieved at not receiving the title, and in 1528 occupied Eresby House in Lincolnshire, which was in the hands of the Crown. Wolsey was called upon to arbitrate, and a solution was reached before Suffolk took over the Crown's interest. His bid was in the air at that point, Sir Christopher was careful not to confront him on the issue, and Suffolk managed to avoid involvement in the dispute.[30] The Duke's careful planning was brought to nothing by the death of Henry in March 1534 at the age of twelve, before any marriage had taken place. However, Mary had also died on 25 June 1533, and the forty-seven-year-old Brandon married the heiress himself in September 1534, and thus secured his hold on her substantial lands in Lincolnshire and Suffolk.

After their return from the Field of Cloth of Gold the Suffolks were frequent but intermittent attenders at the court, dividing their time mostly between their house in Southwark and Westhorpe, which the Queen seems to have regarded as home. The Duke continued to be Henry's chief jousting opponent until 1524, when on 10 March occurred an accident which put him off permanently. The King was trying out a new suit of armour of his own design, and forgot to lower his visor, with the result that when Suffolk's lance shattered, his helmet was filled with splinters. Henry was unhurt, but the Duke was severely shaken and 'sware that he would never run against the king more', with the result that he reverted to his earlier role of being the King's fellow challenger, the Earl of Devon replacing him as Henry's chief opponent.[31] The King and the Duke challenged together in December 1524, disguised in silver beards. However, thereafter they both appeared less frequently, because Henry only chose to run on important occasions, and Brandon appeared only if the King did. When the French ambassadors were to be impressed on 6 May 1527, Henry was due to take part, but did not eventually do so on account of an injury sustained playing tennis, with the result that the Duke did not appear either, and the whole event was scaled down.[32] In spite of his advancing years, he was declared to be in robust health, and danced with the King in November 1527, when he wore three ostrich feathers in his cap, which was mark of especial favour as most of the dancers wore only two! Mary also graced the entertainments of the court, most famously appearing as 'Beauty' in the siege of the Chateau Verte on Shrove Tuesday 1522. On that occasion she had also led the dancing, but by 1527 her dancing days appear to have been over, perhaps on account of her uncertain health, because at thirty-three age can hardly have overtaken her. The new year's gift lists show the couple as consistently in high favour throughout these years, although they were no longer constantly in attendance, and both seem to have resorted to the assiduous Wolsey when it came to promoting the careers of their clients.[33] The Cardinal may have been involved in some grants to the Duke himself, for instance the stewardship of the Duchy of Lancaster in Northern England, which was granted in April 1525 and carried a fee of £100 a year, always welcome to the impecunious Suffolk. He was also an assiduous attender at Garter elections during these years, and even seems to have repaired his relations with the Duke of Norfolk, at least to the extent of reducing the tension over supremacy in East Anglia, which was a sensitive issue to both of them.[34]

As we have seen, the Treaty of the More restored Mary's dower payments. After an interval of three years and nine months, they were duly paid in November 1525, and thereafter every six months. The Queen, however, was not satisfied with the farming arrangement, and tried through Wolsey to gain full control of her dower lands, including the right to appoint her own officers, which seems to have been the main point. Without that right she had no patronage in France, and had a number of French clients whom she wished to reward.[35] One of these was Nicholas de St Martin, who had been her secretary until 1520, when he had been persuaded to enter the service of Francis I. In 1526 Mary got her brother to write to Louise of Savoy asking that he return to her service, and that eventually happened. However St Martin came back to England to his original post, and her attempts to secure control of her lands appear to have come to nothing. Attempts to induce Francis to give the administration of the dower to her servant George Hampton came to nothing, and Hampton was reduced to travelling backwards and forwards on this business, which was quite considerable owing to the extent of the lands.[36] By 1528 he and Mary were working increasingly through Anne de Montmorency, the constable, who was the dominant influence there, but her lack of real influence was exposed by the case of Antoine du Val, who was a clerk in her household, whom she tried unsuccessfully for several months to place in the service of Francis. Montmorency replied politely, but his mind was not on the job, and nothing happened. Du Val turned elsewhere for the necessary patronage, but it is not clear that he succeeded.[37] Mary never entirely got the message, but her attempts to exercise influence in France were thereafter conducted through Cardinal Wolsey, and ceased after his fall in 1529.

Through the summer months of each year, when they were not at court, the Suffolks tended to be peripatetic, visiting their manors in Suffolk, Essex and Oxfordshire on a regular basis. They also visited various towns in East Anglia, such as Great Yarmouth and King's Lynn, where they were received with generous gifts, and royal honours for her.[38] Suffolk in addition undertook occasional and somewhat fleeting trips to his more remote manors in Cheshire and Yorkshire, which were not always welcomed by the men on the spot, but which were necessary to prevent a terminal decline of revenue. They spent weeks at a time at Butley Priory near Bury

St Edmunds, enjoying the hospitality of the canons there in what looks suspiciously like a cost-cutting exercise, because Butley is only a few miles from their principal residence at Westhorpe. Sometimes, when the Duke was about his business, Mary stayed there alone. They put in a regular appearance at the Bury St Edmunds Easter fair every year, bringing prestige, and no doubt additional business while they received the hosts of hopeful clients who invariably followed them there. The Duchess was noted as being particularly gracious on these occasions.[39] All this was necessary for the Duke to maintain his status as a local magnate, and a means of keeping in touch with the gentlemen who formed his natural affinity. It also helped him when he discharged his duty by sitting on county commissions, although his service as a Justice of the Peace was more honoured in the breach than in the observance. In 1524 he was named to the commissions for Middlesex, Berkshire and Oxfordshire as well as for Suffolk, but given his other commitments it is unlikely that he was active in any of them.[40] Because of his position at court, men (and women) appealed to him for help from all over the country, but he seems to have felt a particular obligation to those from his home county. His increasing honour is reflected in the titles accorded to him in the Norwich Episcopal registers. In 1517 he was just 'the Duke of Suffolk', but by 1524 he had become 'the man of vigour, Charles, Duke of Suffolk'. In June 1527 he was 'the most powerful man, Charles Duke of Suffolk, great marshal of England', and by September of that year 'the noble and most powerful prince, Charles Duke of Suffolk and great marshal of England'.[41] These commitments meant that he was often apart from his Duchess, who occupied herself with bringing up her children, running her own clientage network, and undertaking pilgrimages to Walsingham.

Most of this time she spent at Westhorpe, which was an agreeable country retreat where the Duke joined her when he could. There he bred horses, ran a herd of mules, and hunted assiduously in the park, or in nearby Haughey Park. He had purchased the house in 1515, perhaps with a view to his wife's comfort or convenience, and decided in 1527 to rebuild it on a grand scale. It became a brick courtyard house, decorated with terracotta figures and impressive (although totally ornamental) battlements. Work started in that year, and was still not finished in 1538, but the house seems to have been in use throughout, and was managed by Mary, who no doubt filled her days in residence there with the multifarious tasks of a large household.[42] It may have been the pressures of this lifestyle, to say nothing of the need to dodge the building workers, which caused her to take herself off to Butley Priory from time to time. When the subsidy commissioners visited Westhorpe in 1526 they credited Mary with fifty servants, forty-three men and seven women, but these appear to have been the domestic staff only, exclusive of the officers. If Wolsey's comparable assessment is anything to go by, it was a considerable underestimate, and the true figure should have been nearer 100.[43] It was necessary for any early Tudor nobleman to be careful about the number of servants he declared, because of the livery legislation, and although Mary's retinue posed no threat to anyone, she would have been scrupulous to observe the law. Nor would such a list have included the young ladies and gentlemen being brought up in the household. Some of these, like George Heveningham and William Tyrell, were kindred of the Duke, while others such as Elizabeth and Anne Grey had served Mary since her time in France. Altogether there were probably about a dozen of these at any one time, of various ages, some of the younger ones acting as 'schoolfellows' for the Brandon's own children. The Duke himself was credited in 1524 with fifty-one servants, but this was also an underestimate for the same reason. At a time when the Earl of Northumberland kept 166 servants in his livery, and the Duke of Buckingham claimed that it was reasonable for him to travel with an escort of 400, it is unlikely that the Duke of Suffolk retained fewer than 200, which would have included his chapel staff, and the grooms of his stables, as well as the more strictly domestic establishment.[44] In the early 1520s the Duke's household was costing him £1,000 a year in wages and food, which also points to a substantially larger number than the fifty-one declared. It is unlikely that even a great house such as Westhorpe could have accommodated more than a small proportion of this multitude, particularly during the building works, so presumably the rest were either stood down or billeted out in the surrounding villages – which are not numerous in that part of Suffolk.

No inventory survives for Westhorpe, and the only one for Suffolk Place dates from 1535, so it is not easy to judge the style of their housekeeping, but Mary would have found it necessary to retain something of the regal splendour of her days in France, which would not have come cheaply and helps to explain her desperation when her French revenues were suspended. The operational costs of lesser manors, such as Ewelme, were much lower because only a skeleton staff would have resided normally, and the ducal couple would have brought their 'stuff' with them when they visited. Nevertheless, expenditure was not negligible, because gifts and rewards were expected from the Lord and Lady whenever they were there; the neighbours expected to be entertained and the local churches anticipated charitable donations.[45] Hospitality was particularly onerous, because on it depended the Lord's influence in that part of the country, and if the manor was seldom visited, the expectation would have been so much higher. Consequently it only needed a report of the Duke and Duchess' appearance to attract a horde of the expectant and the needy. Figures do not survive for the Suffolks, but their situation would have been similar to that of the Duke of Norfolk at Framlingham in 1526 when he entertained 244 people to dinner, 200 of whom were 'persons of the country'.[46] Life away from the court may have been less stressful, but it was not necessarily much cheaper, and the extravagant lifestyle required by the honour of such a couple constantly outran their resources. When Mary's French revenues arrived on time, they could manage, but at other times their only recourse was to borrow from the King or from the bankers at a rate which neither of them could afford. Hence the constant recourse to Wolsey to renegotiate their agreements with Henry, who preferred to keep them dependant in this fashion rather than granting the Duke adequate lands to provide him with sufficient income. It is not surprising that they welcomed invitations to attend the court, because that provided them both with opportunities to keep their favour bright and fresh, and to remind the King how fond he was of them both.

Another use of Westhorpe was as a house of refuge from the plague and the sweating sickness. Plague was endemic, and many years saw the court on the move to escape its attentions, the King taking his 'riding household' as far afield as Wallingford, Abingdon and Woodstock, because of his deadly fear of infection.[47] The sweat was less lethal, but caused almost equal panic, being particularly severe in 1517 and 1528. 'Multitudes are dying all around us,' Thomas More wrote to Erasmus in the former year; 'almost everyone in Oxford, Cambridge and London has been ill lately'.[48] Nor was the King's fear unreasonable. In 1528 the disease invaded the court, carrying off William Carey and Sir William Compton, the latter as Groom of the Stool, being particularly close to Henry. The medical profession was baffled, and the King came up with his own strange nostrum.

> Take a handful of sage of virtue, and handful of herb grace, and handful of elder leaves and a handful of red briar leaves, and stamp them together, and strain them in a fair cloth with a quart of white wine, and then take a quantity of ginger and mingle them all together, and drink of that medicine a spoonful every day ...[49]

Whether anyone was protected or cured by this concoction we do not know, and it was more usual to resort to prayer or to the offices of the church. Hence perhaps the Duchess of Suffolk's constant visits to Walsingham. However, rural Westhorpe appears to have lived a charmed life, and although the King did not visit it, as far as we know, it provided a safe refuge for the Duke and Duchess. The latter's ill health, which became increasingly obvious after 1525, had nothing to do with these epidemics, the only description which we have of it attributing it to 'her old disease in her side', which could have been a heart condition.[50] The agues from which she also suffered from time to time have been diagnosed as malaria, which clung to the low-lying areas of the Thames valley, but was not usually fatal. The

Duke seems not to have suffered from any of these ailments, but he was still not welcome at court when the fear was on. Only Cardinal Wolsey worked through these epidemics, often falling ill, but always recovering in a manner which the King can only have envied.

8

THE LAST DAYS

After the reception of the French ambassadors in 1527, Mary no longer attended formal public occasions. The Anglo-French treaty in May of that year, and the betrothal of her namesake the princess to the Dauphin, marked her last appearance at a major political event. This was partly due to her health, but had more to do with disillusionment with her brother, who, having expressed the most rigorous disapproval of their sister Margaret's divorce from the Earl of Angus in 1528, was set upon repudiating his own wife.[1] This last was more or less public knowledge after Henry had confronted Catherine in June 1527, and although it was not similarly known that he was intending to replace her with Anne Boleyn, the latter's position was already causing scandal and concern around the court. Mary had been close friends with Catherine since before her marriage to Henry, when they had shared many girlish secrets, and that friendship had not waned over the years. Until 1531 Henry maintained a correct attitude to his wife, dining with her from time to time, while she accompanied him on formal occasions such as the Christmas and Shrovetide celebrations. As long as that situation appertained, the Suffolks continued to appear occasionally together at the court, and were lodged on the Queen's side.² However, in 1531 Henry announced that he never wished to see Catherine again; she was banished to Buckden and the Queen's side of the court was effectively discontinued. When the Duke appeared on his own, he had always been lodged on the King's side, and that continued, but Mary's infrequent appearances were now made from Suffolk Place, or from one of the Duke's other houses if the court was not at Westminster.³

Paradoxically this chill in the relations between brother and sister does not seem to have affected Suffolk's position at all. He had formed an alliance of convenience with the Boleyns and Norfolk in order to get rid of Wolsey, but he did not share their aspirations for Anne's future, and quickly distanced himself from Viscount Rochford (Anne's father) as soon as the Cardinal had been dismissed in October 1529. A more scrupulous man might have withdrawn from the Council while that attack was in hand, because he had much to be grateful to Wolsey for, but he seems to have fallen out with Lord Chancellor over the latter's failure to eliminate his debt repayments, and may indeed have been hoping to take his place. Such a move was rumoured in diplomatic circles before Sir Thomas More was appointed on 26 October.⁴ So instead of withdrawing, or expressing his dissent from the prevailing intention of the Council, he worked closely with the Duke of Norfolk to bring about the desired result. It was the two dukes who went to recover the Great Seal from Wolsey, and the latter does not seem to have been surprised or particularly resentful at the role which he had chosen to play. Norfolk was the senior partner in these manoeuvres, but when the office of President of the Council was revived at this time, it was conferred on the Duke of Suffolk, and this may have been on account of his amicable relations with the French.[5] Norfolk would have preferred an Imperial alliance, but, given Charles's hostile attitude towards the King's annulment proceedings, that was an unrealistic aspiration. The Emperor was Catherine's nephew, and had no intention of permitting such a slur on his family's honour, so given the power structure of contemporary Europe, the assistance of France was more or less essential. Thanks to his marriage, Suffolk had all the right connections in the French court, and given her dependence upon French dowry payments to maintain her standard of living, Mary was in no position to object to his using them in the King's service. When Parliament met on 3 November, the strength of the Duke's position soon became apparent, because many of those elected had links with him, more than was the case with any other senior peer, although only Sir John Shilston, who sat for Southwark, was a direct client.[6] He had taken his share of the spoils after Wolsey's fall; some manors came to him, and the Cardinal's prize train of mules, but he resisted the temptation to urge any expropriation of the Church, and in that the King supported him rather than listening to the voices of the Boleyns, whose influence in that direction was to be delayed for several years. By 1530 the Duke of Suffolk and his influence were everywhere to be seen, but his actual power remained problematical, perhaps due to a lack of ambition – or perhaps to a lack of ability for government at the highest level.

He was present everywhere, but it is hard to pinpoint what he actually did. For example, he was a prominent member of the court which tried Wolsey, but made no distinctive contribution to its deliberations, and although he was present at Lord

Rochford's elevation to the earldom of Wiltshire in December 1529, his role was purely that of a spectator. In December he helped, as a member of the Council, in the entertainment of the French and Imperial envoys, and was privately, but somewhat ineffectually, courted by the former, who of course knew about his connections. When Wolsey began scheming to regain favour in the early part of 1530, he bypassed the Duke altogether, preferring to deal directly with his real antagonists, Norfolk and the Boleyns.[7] Since the Cardinal was a shrewd judge of political realities, we must assume that Suffolk was not an important cog in the machinery of government. It was not that he had become a nonentity. Petitioners from the country continued to approach him with small bribes and requests for help, but he had no personal or ideological axe to grind, and may well have found the politics of 1530 and 1531 baffling. Whenever called upon to do so, he made supportive noises in the King's cause, promoted his policy with ambassadors, and was suitably rude about the Pope. However, there is no sign of real conviction about any of these activities, and his conversations were more likely to be held at dinner or in the Privy Chamber rather than in the Council, at which his attendance was so erratic that his nominal presidency never really took effect.[8] He sat on the commissions which examined and tried Fisher and More in 1535, but did not ask pertinent questions, and although he was commissioned to oversee the tricky matter of a peacetime subsidy in the country, the only outcome was the receipt of the Stewardship of Oxford town in that same year. In March 1534 the Venetian ambassador did not think that he was worth bribing, and did not name him among those leading personages whom the King most trusted to negotiate a new marriage alliance with France.[9] It may well have been that his own lack of energy and application were responsible for this situation, because his friendship with Henry appears to have remained intact. They played bowls and gambled together, but when the King wanted serious business discharged, he now looked to Thomas Cromwell, and the Duke became one of Cromwell's many clients.

It may even have been that he found his role in the court distasteful, torn as he was between loyalty to the King and disagreement with his policies. On 16 June 1531 Eustace Chapuys wrote to the Emperor:

> Suffolk and his wife, if they dared, would offer all possible resistance to this marriage [between Henry and Anne], and it is not two days since he and the Treasurer [the Duke of Norfolk], talking of this matter, agreed that now the time was come when all the world should try to dissuade the king from his folly ...[10]

Chapuys is not an altogether reliable witness, because of his commitment to Catherine and his tendency to hear what he wanted to hear. For instance, in 1530 he reported that Suffolk was out of favour because he had drawn to Henry's attention that Anne had had an affair with Sir Thomas Wyatt in the 1520s, for neither of which statement is there any corroboratory evidence. However, the above observation is sufficiently consistent with what else we know about the Brandons' attitude to carry conviction. Suffolk found his role in the progressive demotion of Catherine uncongenial. In April 1533 he was entrusted with the task of informing her that she was no longer Queen, following Cranmer's decision on her marriage, and the following December was ordered to relocate her to Somersham, and to dismiss some of her servants, because she was now the Dowager Princess of Wales, and could not maintain a regal establishment.[11] In fact Henry was not ungenerous to his ex-wife, and her reconstituted household cost him some £3,000 a year, but Suffolk was not to know that, and Lady Mary Willoughby, by then his mother-in-law, told Chapuys that he had confessed and communicated before setting off on this mission, hoping for some accident to prevent its completion – or at least that is what the ambassador said.[12] When Catherine died in January 1536, Suffolk's youngest daughter Eleanor was the chief mourner, supported by his new Duchess, Catherine Willoughby. Understandably Anne Boleyn was consistently hostile to the couple. In July 1531 she actually accused the Duke of having sexual relations with his own daughter, a charge which only the King's intervention prevented from escalating into a major quarrel. There was an actual affray within the court in April 1532, which resulted in the death of one of Suffolk's gentlemen, and the Venetian report of the incident went on:

> It is said to have been caused by a private quarrel, but I am assured that it was owing to opprobrious language uttered against Madame Anne by his Majesty's sister, the Duchess of Suffolk, Queen Dowager of France …[13]

However, Anne herself could only swallow her indignation when the King decided to ignore these slights, and visit the Suffolks at Westhorpe, which he did towards the end of July 1532. Presumably she did not accompany him on this visit! On 1 September, when he conferred on Anne the title of Marquis of Pembroke, Mary was conspicuous by her absence. On 7 September Carlo Capello, the Venetian envoy, reported that when Henry crossed to Calais to meet with King Francis, he would be accompanied by 'Madame Anne' and thirty of the chief ladies of the realm, led by the Duchess of Norfolk, but that the King's sister, the widow of King Louis of France, had 'stoutly refused to go'.[14] Her absence was intended, and was construed as, a snub to Anne, but it was also a reflection on the King's honour, which he chose to ignore. Mary's health by that time was so uncertain that excuses were easy to make, and in any case he was so pleased by the outcome of his meeting that he probably chose to overlook the slight.

At the Treaty of the More it had been agreed that the payment of Mary's dower revenues would be resumed, and that appears to have happened, because at the end of 1526 an indenture was drawn up between the King and his sister 'with her husband the Duke of Suffolk' for the repayment of their outstanding debt. This was assessed at £19,333 for the expenses of Mary's marriage to Louis, and £6,519 for various sums lent to the Duke, and for revenues received and not accounted for. They agreed to pay £1,000 a year in half yearly instalments, two-thirds being for her debt and one-third for his.[15] If she died, her outstanding debt would be cancelled, but her jewels and hangings were to be returned to the King. If there were to be any further interruption to her revenues from France, then her repayments were to be suspended until they were resumed. For the time being the payments were being made at the rate of 17,300 livres (about £3,000) per year, but at some time early in 1531 Montmorency, with Francis's agreement, apparently promised an increase to 20,000 (£3,800). On 18 April Suffolk wrote to Montmorency to remind him of this promise, and was assured that the increase would take effect in the following financial year, it being too late to make the adjustment to current payments.[16] Negotiations continued, and at the end of July de la Barre, the Provost of Paris, sent the Bishop of Amiens to the Duchess 'touching her dowry', presumably to reassure her that it would be paid. This was not a regular diplomatic mission, and according to Chapuys the Bishop went straight to the Duchess's lodgings, and then returned immediately to France, without paying his respects at the court.[17] There may have been other such private visits which have gone unrecorded. It was a sensitive issue, and one of vital concern to the Suffolks, so that the Duke kept up his contacts with Montmorency for that purpose. For that reason, Brandon was sent on various missions to France during these years, in which he no doubt combined official business with his own private concerns.

At New Year 1533 the Brandons as usual exchanged gifts with the King, although Mary was by then a sick woman. Nevertheless she kept up her intercessions for those who appealed to her for help, writing several time to Lord Lisle, the Governor of Calais, for places which were within his gift. The last such letter was written on 30 March in favour of one John Williams. It was written, as usual, by a secretary, but was signed in what the calendar notes as 'a very shaky hand'.[18] On the whole she had more success with her pleas than the Duke did. Only those whose information was inadequate or outdated tended to appeal to him directly by this time. Admittedly the Earl of Cumberland was one who requested his intercession with the King, but the Duke thought it wise to pass the letter to Cromwell, whose influence with Henry was now markedly greater than his own. His relations with the Secretary were surprisingly good, perhaps more a sign of Cromwell's tact than his own flexibility, and his dependants frequently appealed to Cromwell for help, with Brandon's approval. When they clashed over patronage, the Duke was firm but apologetic, and this seems to have been acceptable to the chief minister. They occasionally hunted together, but were never personally close, and Suffolk reacted angrily in 1532 when Cromwell passed on to the King some slanderous rumours which were circulating about him.[19] Theirs was a working relationship because the minister knew perfectly well that it would take more than a few rumours to unseat the Duke from a relationship which went back before the beginning of the reign. On 1 June 1533 Anne Boleyn was crowned, and Suffolk was once again called upon to perform an uncongenial duty. He was High Steward and Constable for the day, and since the Duke of Norfolk was away on a diplomatic mission, he had the highlight pretty much to himself – after the Queen, that is, whom no effort was spared to make appear rather more than mortal. He presided over the Court of Claims which preceded the coronation, and over the table of peers at the subsequent banquet.[20] The Duchess did not appear, but given her state of health no one was surprised by that, no doubt to the Duke's relief. The princess Mary (now the Lady Mary) also did not appear at the celebration of her mother's rival, and that was not commented upon either, but several observers noted the absence of the Duchess of Norfolk, who in the absence of the French Queen should have led the peeresses. Suffolk, however, had one thing on his mind which was not connected with the day's events, because before he departed on his mission the Duke of Norfolk had requested that he hand over his office of Earl Marshall. Only the King could effect such a change, and Henry accepted Norfolk's case, requesting Suffolk to stand down in terms that could not be denied. He innocently declared himself pleased that Brandon had shown 'zeal to nourish kindness and love' with the senior duke, knowing perfectly well that he had no option.[21] The evidence suggests that Suffolk surrendered his position with an ill grace, and that the change did nothing to increase the 'kindness and love' between them, as Norfolk was warned during June. The office conferred no status that the Duke did not already possess, and the fee was minimal, but it did stand at the head of the chivalric hierarchy in England, and of the heralds and Kings of Arms, and that conferred a prestige which Suffolk took seriously, hence his disgruntlement over his forced resignation.

During the last years of her life, Mary spent most of her time at Westhorpe, while her family steadily dwindled around her. Anne was married in 1525 and Mary in 1527 or 1528, and although they remained in sense dependent upon the Duke, their membership of the Duchess's household ceased at that point. Frances was married in London in 1531, an event which tempted Mary out of her seclusion, and only fourteen-year-old Eleanor remained at home when she succumbed to her final illness.[22] In spite of her disillusionment over Henry's treatment of Catherine, her affection for her brother was clearly undimmed. Several months earlier she had written to him as her 'Most dearest and best beloved brother'.

I humbly commend myself to your grace ... I have been very sick and ill at ease, for which I was fain to send for Master Peter the physician for to have holpen me of this disease which I have, howbeit I am rather worse than better, wherefore I trust surely to come to London with my Lord. For if I should tarry here I should never asperge the sickness [and] I would be glad to see your grace the which I do think long for to do. For I have been a great while out of your sight [which is] the greatest comfort to me that may be possible …[23]

Whether she realised her ambition on that occasion is not known, nor whether it produced any amelioration in her condition. By May 1533 it was clearly too late for any such therapy. Early in the month the Duke made a hasty visit to Westhorpe to see her, but it was to be the last time that he would do so. Preoccupied with the coronation and its aftermath, and perhaps sceptical of the alarming reports emanating from Westhorpe, he did not appear again before she died on 25 June. As far as we know, only Eleanor and Henry were with her at the time, and we have no evidence of the details.[24] She had been in a fragile state for some time, but there is no indication that her condition was thought to be terminal. Nor do we know anything of the competence of the physicians who attended her, although they were presumably in the Duke's employment. The Spanish Chronicle attributed her death to grief over Henry's behaviour, 'the sight of her brother leaving his wife brought on an illness of which she died', but that was voice out of Catherine's camp, willing to attribute every ill to Anne Boleyn, and need not be taken seriously.[25] Perhaps the most likely explanation is angina. In spite of her relative youth (she was thirty-eight) it was several years since she had cut a dash on the courtly scene, and her political opinions, although well known, were important only insofar as they influenced those of her husband. Henry seems to have been genuinely although briefly distressed, and the court went into official mourning, but no one else apart from her family was particularly concerned. A French envoy, writing to Francis I, reported her death on the 27th, and wrote again on the 30th, commenting that she was 'much beloved in the country and by the common people of [London]'.[26] This no doubt had something to do with the generosity of her largesse, but was probably more on account of her well-known sympathy with Queen Catherine, who had a large popular following.

Mary's body was embalmed, and lay in state in the chapel at Westhorpe for over three weeks before burial. Her passing bell had been heard just before eight o'clock on the morning of her death, but the rituals had to be carefully observed for one of her status, and the length of the delay was probably caused by the time which it took for a delegation to come from France.[27] Meanwhile a wax chandler had 'sered and trammelled' the body with spiced cloth, which was then sealed in a leaden box covered with black velvet and adorned with a cross of white damask. While it was still in the chapel the coffin was covered with an embroidered pall of blue velvet, many tapers burned day and night and a continuous vigil was kept by the members of her household. A detailed account of her funeral is preserved among the manuscripts of the College of Arms, which shows that all the preparations were complete by 20 July.[28] English heralds arrived from London to accompany the French pursuivants, and black gowns, hoods and trains had been issued to all the aristocratic participants. Neither the King nor the Duke were present, the chief mourner being her daughter Frances, who was escorted by her husband the Marquis of Dorset, and by her brother the Earl of Lincoln. Ladies Powis and Mounteagle were also present, Eleanor, and Catherine Willoughby the Duke's ward who had been living in the house. The interment was to be in the abbey church at Bury St Edmunds, and for the journey thither the coffin was placed on a hearse draped in black velvet emblazoned with Mary's arms, and covered with a pall of black cloth of gold, betokening the wealth of the deceased. On this lay Mary's effigy, representing her as Queen of France, complete with robes of state, a gold crown and a golden sceptre as a symbol of her (supposed) power. It is not known whether this effigy was of wax or carved wood, and in any case it has long since disappeared, but it was presumably designed by a well-known artist of the time, possibly the King's Sergeant Painter, Andrew Wright.[29] The hearse on its journey was drawn by six horses, trapped in black cloth, while over it was a canopy borne by four knights of the Duke's affinity. Alongside it were more standard bearers carrying the insignia of the Brandon and Tudor families. The whole cortège was led by a hundred torch bearers, who were local country folk recruited for the occasion, given coarse blacks and few pence for their trouble, and who were followed by the clergy bearing the chapel cross. Next came the household staff, heralds and officials suitably mounted, followed by the hearse, and then the knights and nobles in attendance. After them came another hundred taper bearers, only in this case they were the Duke's yeomen, which must have left the Duke, who remained at Ewelme, 'but thinly attended'. The cortège was completed by the female mourners, led by the Marchioness of Dorset, the mounted ladies, two mourning wagons or coaches containing those unable or unwilling to ride, and Mary's waiting women and other servants on foot. Along the way, we are told, others joined the procession, because Mary was well thought of in the county, and many wished to pay their respects. Representatives of neighbouring parishes met the procession at intervals, were given torches and money, and followed on behind. Bury St Edmunds was reached at about two o'clock in the afternoon, and the body was received by the abbot and monks of the abbey.[30] The coffin was placed on a catafalque before the high altar, and surrounded by the mourners in strict order of precedence. The dirge was then sung, and the French pursuivant commended the soul of the 'right high excellent princess, and right Christian Queen' to the prayers of the assembled company.

That completed the proceedings for that day, and everyone moved to the monastic refectory, where a supper had been 'plenteously prepared'. There was food and drink for everyone, but the abbey could only accommodate so many guests, so whereas the nobles and officials were provided for, presumably the rest either went home or found such lodgings as might be available in the town. Eight women, twelve men, thirty yeomen and a number of clergy were appointed to watch about the corpse during the night, probably in shifts, and accommodation was no doubt provided for those, either within the abbey or nearby. Early the next morning breakfast was served, in the refectory for important visitors and elsewhere for the others, and the ceremonies were resumed at about seven o'clock. A requiem mass was sung, and the six leading mourners, the four Suffolk daughters, Catherine Willoughby and her mother, offered their palls of cloth of gold at the altar. The funeral oration was delivered by William Rugg, at that time Abbot of St Benet's at Hulme in Norfolk, and soon (June 1536) to be Bishop of Norwich, who may well have been a client of Mary's at an earlier stage in his career.[31] It was a long and wearying address, and so exhausted were Frances and Eleanor after listening to it that they were excused attendance at the actual inhumation. This, which took place within the abbey church as became her rank, was attended by the other mourners and by all Mary's officers, who broke their staves into the grave, as the custom was. On the following day, which was 23 July, the funeral party dispersed, the family returning to Westhorpe. Mary was long remembered in Suffolk as a gracious lady, and the memory was reinforced by the great dole which was distributed after the final funeral dinner on the 22nd, when meat and drink had been available to all, and every poor person had received four pennies. An alabaster monument was erected in the church, but was destroyed at the dissolution just a few years later, and the details and cost of its construction have also disappeared.[32] At that time the coffin was also removed to the neighbouring church of St Marys, where it still is. It has been twice opened, and fragments of her hair removed, but in 1784 it was reinterred in the chancel at St Mary's, and the grave covered with the original slab of Petworth marble which had marked her altar tomb in the abbey church. Since the end of the eighteenth century she has been allowed to rest in peace.

While Mary still lay in state at Westhorpe, her brother and husband had solemnised another funeral service for her at Westminster Abbey.[33] It was presumably by her own wish that she had been buried at Bury St Edmunds, and neither the King nor the Duke had found it possible to be present, but she had been a great lady, with a high profile at court, and a proper tribute to her rank and virtue was called for. It took place on 10 and 11 July with all the ostentatious formality accorded to royalty. That had not been a feature of the ceremony at Bury, in spite of its magnificence, her royal status only being recognised in the presence of the French heralds. At Westminster the Earl of Essex led seven delegated mourners, with the Kings of Arms, heralds and pursuivants all performing their official duties, and the ceremony was the same except that it did not have an actual body to focus upon. Presumably the breaking of staves was also omitted as there would have been no grave, and in any case Mary's officers were all in Suffolk at the time. The London obsequies were presumably paid for by the King, who observed that Mary was a queen worthy of such expenditure, but the Suffolk funeral expenses were met by the Duke.[34] In the absence of any household accounts we have no idea how much it cost, but in view of the quantities of food and drink consumed, to say nothing of the doles, and the amount of black cloth which needed to be provided, it must have run to many hundreds of pounds.[35] The Duke as usual was hard up and heavily in debt, and the termination of Mary's dower payments must have been a real headache to him. Inevitably he stood down most of her household, but he still had two unmarried children and his ward to support, as well as the regular expenses of his own household. Fortunately Henry again came to the rescue, remitting £1,000 of his debt to the Crown, and granting him the fruits of the vacant see of Ely for the year 1533/34, which would have amounted to over £2,000.[36] Brandon was also capable of helping himself in this situation, and within three months he had remarried, his bride being his ward Catherine Willoughby, who had been originally purchased for his son. Henry, however, was only eleven, which would have meant a wait of three years, and Suffolk's problems were pressing. Catherine was fourteen and apparently willing to become the next Duchess of Suffolk, so they were married on 7 September. Mary had been in her grave only seven weeks, and many disapproving observations were made, but the Duke urgently needed a source of revenue to replace that which his deceased wife had provided, and

Catherine was well endowed both in Lincolnshire and in East Anglia.

He commenced his new married life with a series of legal tussles with his wife's uncle, Sir Christopher Willoughby, tussles which were fronted by the Dowager Lady Willoughby. The two of them, acting in collusion, obtained a writ of *supersedeas* to prevent Sir Christopher having inquisitions held on all the late Lord William's estates, and the issue was eventually resolved by an arbitration before the King which resulted in Suffolk retaining his control over the bulk of the Lincolnshire lands in his wife's name.[37] However, Mary's death necessitated a fresh financial settlement between the King and the Duke, and Henry (or Brian Tuke on his behalf) pulled no punches. By the summer of 1535 it had been agreed that the Queen's outstanding debt should be cancelled, but that left Suffolk to pay £6,700. He handed over jewels to the value of £4,360, and agreed an unfavourable exchange of lands with the King. He lost all his Oxfordshire and Berkshire manors, including Ewelme, valued at £480 a year, in return for ex-Percy land in Lincolnshire worth £175 a year, £2,333 in cash and the cancellation of his remaining debts.[38] He was also forced to surrender the reversion of his new house at Westhorpe for a Percy manor in Essex and £850 in cash. It was not until November of that year that this settlement was complete, his title to the Lincolnshire lands secured, and his and the Queen's debts finally written off. Even then he had to give up Suffolk Place in Southwark in return for a London house recently surrendered by the Bishop of Norwich as a part of the price for his installation.[39] When he took stock of his financial situation early in 1535, apart from his debt to the Crown, which was still alive at that point, he had liabilities of £2,415 and assets of £2,210 in the form of debts due from sundry creditors. His income from all sources at this time can be roughly gauged from a subsidy assessment of 1534, which shows it at £2,000 'clear', that is after allowances and deductions.[40] Since it was customary for peers to be under-assessed, this probably indicates a real revenue of between £2,500 and £3,000, which would be about right for a peer of his status.

Mary's death of course led to the sequestration of her French revenues, which was ordered by Francis I on 7 July 1533, as soon as news of the event reached him. It remained only to tidy up her accounts by paying to Suffolk such arrears as were still outstanding.[41] George Hampton busied himself with this until his death late in 1534, after which the Duke was compelled to rely on Nicholas de St Martin, with the result that by September 1535 the payments were four months overdue. Suffolk did his best to keep up pressure via Montmorency, but this was not effective and his contacts with the French court gradually languished.[42] His French pension was only half that of the Duke of Norfolk, and Anne Boleyn's French contacts discouraged his further efforts. He had been in receipt of an Imperial pension since 1529, and by 1536 Chapuys detected clear signs of movement on his part in favour of an Imperial alliance.[43] Such a move was of course facilitated by the death of Catherine of Aragon in January, and even more by the fall of Anne Boleyn in May, an event not a little connected with Thomas Cromwell's pro-Imperial policies. By July the Duke was voicing the opinion that there was no greater a Turk than the King of France, a sentiment prompted by the Franco-Ottoman understanding of that year. Suffolk's influence in court and in Council was recovering by the summer of 1536 on the basis of his Imperial connections after the setback marked by the King's harsh dealings over his financial affairs.

Also, following the death of the Earl of Lincoln on 1 March 1534, which had left him without a male heir, his new marriage proved fruitful. On 18 September 1535 Catherine gave birth to a son, who was again hopefully named Henry, and to whom the King and Thomas Cromwell stood as godfathers.[44] In the two years which followed the French Queen's death, her husband had re-orientated himself completely. Gone was his pro-French stance in the Council, and his dependence on French money. Gone too, was his local influence in Oxfordshire and Berkshire, to be replaced by a move to Lincolnshire following the rearrangement of his estates. He had also settled his financial differences with the King and formed an alliance of convenience with Thomas Cromwell, with the result that his friendship with Henry revived. It was based now on bowls and cards rather than on tennis and jousting, but above all it was based on long memories. The King did not have many friends as opposed to servants, and his affection for Brandon blossomed in the new circumstances.

9

THE LEGACY

The Willoughby lands in Lincolnshire had been divided by Lord William's death, part going to Suffolk with Catherine's wardship, and part remaining as the dower lands of his widow, Lady Mary. The Duke consequently did not control the latter until Lady Willoughby died in 1539, although he worked in close collaboration with her to fend off the assaults of Sir Christopher, the late lord's brother.[1] In fact, observing the terms of Lord William's will, and paying the Crown £100 a year for his outstanding debts, can have left her little to contribute to Catherine's well-being – nor is there any evidence that she did so. Suffolk, however, controlled several manors in Lincolnshire apart from his wife's inheritance, and was reckoned to be 'a great inheritor in those parts', a description which he might not have recognised in 1535. In 1535 also he negotiated a successful marriage for his younger daughter by the French Queen when the seventeen-year-old Eleanor was wedded to Henry Clifford, the son and heir of the Earl of Cumberland.[2] If this reduced his outgoings it was only briefly, because on 18 September of the same year his new wife bore him a son, which necessitated the establishment of a fresh nursery with its complement of staff. The child was named for the King, who as we have seen stood godfather, so what was lost in financial terms was gained in honour.

When rebellion broke out in Lincolnshire in October 1536, it was therefore natural for Henry to turn to his friend Charles Brandon to act as his lieutenant in those parts, although he could hardly be described as a locally based magnate. After careful consultations with the Duke of Norfolk and the Earl of Oxford, he decided that the urgency of the situation required immediate action, and set off with only his riding household.[3] It may be that he was already aware that most of the so-called gentry leaders of the rebels were at best half-hearted about their cause, and had decided to play on their reluctance in negotiation. He used a stick-and-carrot technique, agreeing to intercede for their pardons on the condition that they advanced no further. If they persisted on the other hand, he would have no option but to fight. This attempt to buy time was successful. By the time that the rebels had agreed to disperse and sue for pardon, he had been joined by Sir John Russell and Sir William Parr with 3,000 fighting men and sixteen guns.[4] In these circumstances when the Earl of Shrewsbury sent a herald to Lincoln, there was no will to resist, and the gentlemen rode to Stamford to submit to the Duke. Suffolk's commission now required him to investigate the circumstances of the Lincolnshire revolt, and this he did by interrogating some of the surrendered gentlemen, who naturally blamed the intransigence of the commons, a few of whose leaders they actually handed over. When he entered Lincoln, suitably guarded, on 16 October, the reaction of the crowd appeared to vindicate this explanation.[5] He was also instructed to support Shrewsbury further north in Yorkshire, and that was not altogether consistent with what he was expected to do at Lincoln, because to have denuded himself of troops would have been to invite renewed disturbances, a point which the King took when he instructed him to proceed to 'severe justice' against the guilty parties. The situation in the county remained confused. On 17 October it was reported that the beacons were burning again in Louth, but ten days later Sir John Russell entered the town without resistance and disarmed the inhabitants, who were nevertheless described as 'very hollow'. Suffolk proceeded cautiously in disarming the other towns, first receiving the submissions of the gentry and civic leaders, and imprisoning whoever they presented. Contingents of troops were sent to collect the surrendered arms.[6] The Duke moved with similar caution in conducting his enquiries. He filled Lincoln Castle with prisoners, but very few of them were subsequently executed, and he was constantly distracted by developments in Yorkshire. Once Norfolk's and Shrewsbury's armies had withdrawn under the terms of the Doncaster truce of 27 October, the north of Lincolnshire had to be properly defended, and by late November he had 3,600 men deployed for that purpose. Meanwhile Suffolk, who was not bound by the Doncaster truce, maintained an army of spies in Yorkshire, and planned to mobilise 5,000 men for an attack upon Hull which never materialised.[7] On 16 November his work in Lincolnshire culminated in the issue of the expected royal pardon, and on the 27th he mustered the whole county under the leadership of its gentlemen to go against the Yorkshire rebels, a contingency which did not arise owing to the Pontefract agreement of 4 December.[8]

Suffolk's role in these events firmly established him as the new leader of Lincolnshire society, and restored his intimate relations with the King, with whom he exchanged letters more fulsome than any which had been seen in recent years. The Pontefract pardon took effect; the Pilgrims dispersed and the Duke's troops were disbanded. He and the Duchess were invited to spend the Christmas at court. It is not certain that he got there for the festive season because it was 24 December before his deputy arrived to take over, and 18 January 1537 before we have any clear evidence of his presence with the King. When he left the court in April, Henry instructed him to make his main residence in Lincolnshire, and gave him Tattershall Castle for that purpose.[9] As a result of the traumatic events of the Pilgrimage of Grace, Suffolk had been transformed from an East Anglian magnate into a Lincolnshire one, to be at the King's command as he had been previously. Once there, he wasted no time in mobilising his affinity, and incorporating into it the existing Willoughby clientage, with the full co-operation of Lady Willoughby, who realised which side her bread was buttered. Perhaps because her health was failing, Suffolk appears increasingly to have been managing her affairs during 1538, appointing to church livings in her gift and mobilising the Willoughby affinity for his own purposes. Mary kept nominal control, signing a court roll as late as 7 May 1539, but by the 20th she was dead and the Duke was suing for livery of her lands. These were formally granted to him in July 1540, and that gave him another £900 of income.[10] In addition his favour with the King led to significant grants of ex-monastic property. He sued for these lands in the customary fashion, and they were given to him in two tranches in December 1538 and March 1539. A few years later they were bringing in £1,650 a year, and must have increased his revenue by about 30 per cent. Such lands were mostly in Lincolnshire also, and those that were outside the county he sold or exchanged. These transactions, together with his existing holdings, made him the greatest landowner in the county, and gave him a special role in its government, a role which his good relations with Thomas Cromwell merely served to reinforce.

Meanwhile his family was causing problems. Not, it should added, the Duchess Catherine, who discharged her duties, both at court in attendance on Anne of Cleves and Catherine Howard and as lady bountiful in Lincolnshire with impeccable fortitude. She also presented Charles with a second son in 1537 who was named for his father and about whose early years virtually nothing is known.[11] The trouble was with his two elder daughters, Anne, Lady Powis and Mary, Lady Mouteagle. Anne took a lover, who was violently ejected from her lodgings by Lord Powis in a night raid. A legal separation inevitably followed for which Cromwell negotiated the maintenance agreement. Rather surprisingly, Lady Powis continued to be *persona grata* at court, borrowing the necessary cash from Cromwell or from her father. Lord Powis died on 2 July 1551, and his widow (as she still was) remarried Randolph Hayward, although whether he was her earlier lover is not known.[12] Tensions between Lord and Lady Mounteagle also exacerbated their problems, but these were basically caused by Thomas's incompetence. In February 1538 he still owed the Duke over £1,000, and in order to cancel this debt Suffolk arranged to take over the custody and marriage of his son William in return for £100 worth of land. This was not the only problem and in July 1540 Lord Mounteagle was bound to keep the terms of an arbitration between himself and the Duke which had been negotiated by the Crown surveyor, and which may well have related to the same lands.[13] Fortunately the marriages of his two younger daughters seem to have worked out well.

They were beautiful, like their mother, but this seems to have caused no problems. So, apart from the fact that Suffolk believed that Lord Clifford and Eleanor were living in an unhealthy house, there were no issues between them. There is no reason to suppose that her death at the age of twenty-eight in 1547 was connected with this particular concern. It is much more likely to have been caused by childbearing. Both marriages were fruitful, but the sons died young, leaving a problem with which Edward VI had to deal in due course. Outside the immediate family, the move from Suffolk to Lincolnshire seems to have caused some fellow nobles to hesitate before placing their daughters in such a remotely located household. Lady Lisle, for instance, although on good terms with the Duchess, and in spite of the best efforts of the Earl of Shrewsbury, eventually declined the honour.[14] The Suffolks themselves, however, seem to have taken to northern society with aplomb, but then they were spending a considerable amount of time at court, where the Duke had been created Lord Great Master of the Household in 1539. This was a new office, intended by Cromwell to replace both the Lord Steward and the Lord Chamberlain, which it did for a few years, until the Lord Chamberlainship was reinstated in 1543.[15]

In the government of the realm, as distinct from the locality, Suffolk was reasonably assiduous during these years. He attended about 80 per cent of the meetings of the House of Lords, and in the absence of both Norfolk and Audley took the Chancellor's place as the director of business. He was prominent on ceremonial occasions, was a leading judge in the treason trials of 1538 and 1539, and was careful always to reflect the King's opinion on any issue of controversy.[16] As Lord Great Master he disposed considerable patronage within the Household, and a number of his clients found places in the newly constituted band of Gentlemen Pensioners, which was formed also in 1539. He was a leading negotiator with Anne of Cleves, and her tame surrender owed a good deal to his tactful handling of what could have been a very difficult situation. He was not a party to the overthrow of Thomas Cromwell in the summer of 1540, and did not challenge Norfolk for the primacy in Council which followed the chief minister's fall. His relations with Cromwell had always been good, but he was not foolish enough to rush to his defence, having read the King's mind accurately. His power was private rather than public, and depended once again upon his relationship with Henry, but it increased considerably between 1536 and 1540, largely because of his successful handing of the Lincolnshire revolt. When he did return to the public arena, it was in a military capacity. A proposed expedition to defend Calais in August 1542 came to nothing, but in October and November of that year he defended the Anglo-Scottish border while Norfolk carried out the harrying raids which resulted in the Scottish defeat at the Battle of Solway Moss in November, and from January 1543 to March 1544 served as the King's Lieutenant in the North of England.[17] In that capacity he worked closely with John Dudley, Viscount Lisle, who was Lord Warden of the Marches, and to whom it fell to conduct the difficult relations with the Scottish regency government which followed the death of James V in December. There is some evidence to suggest that Suffolk resented being used in an administrative capacity, and that he would dearly have loved to lead an invasion of Scotland himself, but such was the King's will, and he had to be satisfied, perhaps having been reassured that he would be given a suitable command when the King invaded France, which he was planning to do once the Scottish situation had been resolved.

As war with France grew closer, Suffolk's assiduity in Council increased because Henry relied increasingly upon his advice, and from July to November 1544 he commanded the King's own ward in the Army Royal which he led to the siege of Boulogne.[18] Although he was by this time sixty years of age, his health seems to have been bearing up remarkably well, and he was given the whole responsibility for setting up the siege. This was potentially a tricky assignment, because it was intended as a public relations exercise as well as a military one, and had to be so laid that once the King himself appeared on the scene he would be assured of a swift victory and a triumphant entry into the conquered town. Rather surprisingly, it all worked according to plan, and while Norfolk and Russell were bogged down in the siege of Montreuil, Boulogne surrendered. On 14 September the King was able to take possession of his conquest.[19]

Suffolk had been far more than a nominal commander of this operation. He had personally and at some risk supervised the placement of the batteries; he had taken the outlying defences and commenced mining operations, and his retinue had been heavily involved in the skirmishing which had accompanied these operations. Until the King's arrival he also presided over the council of war, and dealt with ambassadors and messengers, working closely with the King's secretary William Paget.[20] After Henry had carried out his state entry and returned home, Suffolk was appointed to go to the relief of Norfolk and Russell. However, before he could do so, Charles V had abandoned his ally and signed a separate peace with France, which meant that all the Imperial troops and most of the mercenaries withdrew from the campaign, leaving the two dukes to extricate themselves as best they could. The French advance on 1 October precluded a return to Boulogne, and they beat an undignified retreat to Calais. This was done with the agreement of Viscount Lisle, who had been left in charge of the conquered town, but Henry was furious, mainly with the Emperor for abandoning his campaign, but temporarily with Norfolk and Suffolk as well, until their predicament was explained to him.[21] He then asked Suffolk to stay on at Calais, and return to the relief of Boulogne if necessary. However, the French retreated and by the end of November the Duke was back in London. In spite of Henry's brief discontent, the 1544 campaign brought Suffolk honour and profit, the latter in the form of the lands of Tattershal College which he was permitted to purchase at a concessionary rate. At £2,666 the price was less than eight years' value, whereas the standard rate was twenty years.[22] However, he can have spent but little time in Lincolnshire because in 1545 he was named as the King's Lieutenant in the South and South East of England, and busied himself both with assembling troops to resist the threatened French invasion and in preparing a counter-strike across the Channel. He continued active almost to the last, sitting in Council just a week before his death, which occurred at Guildford Manor on 22 August 1545. At the time of his death his estates were valued at a little over £3,000 a year. In spite of the financial problems which he had encountered over the years, thanks to the King's patronage he still contrived to die a rich man.[23]

His religious beliefs appear to have been on the conservative side, but he played no active part in the disputes which divided the court and Council on that issue in the 1540s. The six chaplains who appeared at his funeral went in different directions over the next few years, and his will is ambiguous. However, it does seem that he employed and patronised men of more radical views than his own, and he was mourned as a supporter of the gospel by the religious exiles who had taken refuge from the Act of Six Articles on the Continent.[24] It seems that this was partly due to his well-known dislike of Bishop Stephen Gardiner, and partly to the evangelical tendencies of his Duchess. Catherine was conventionally pious, as he was, but increasingly from 1540 onwards filled their houses at Tattershall and Grimesthorpe with protestant sympathisers, one of whom, Alexander Seton, was disciplined for a radical sermon in 1541.[25] Her close association with Queen Catherine Parr after 1543 moved her further in the same direction, and the death of the Duke seems to have freed her from whatever inhibitions that relationship had imposed upon her. In June 1546 she was accused of supporting the imprisoned Protestant Anne Askew, and at the beginning of the following year was named by Chapuys as one of the Queen's most dangerous friends.[26] She was said to rule Lincolnshire through her clientage network, but most of her time when not at court must have been spent in bringing up her two sons, both of whom died as adolescents in Cambridge in 1551. At that point the Brandon Suffolk title became extinct, and the dignity was conferred on Frances's husband, Henry Grey, Marquis of Dorset, in October of that year. In 1552 the thirty-three-year-old widowed Duchess married her Chamberlain, Richard Bertie, and the pair of them went into exile as soon as the papal authority was restored at the beginning of 1555. After a somewhat traumatic journey through North Germany, they ended up as guests of the King of Poland, and their son (the appropriately named Peregrine) was born during their exile.[27] They returned on Mary's death, and seem to have enjoyed good relations with William Cecil. On the other hand their increasing Puritanism distanced them from the Queen, and Catherine never became intimate with Elizabeth. Instead she confined her attentions increasingly to Lincolnshire, where she and her husband enjoyed significant influence in spite of the fact that he held no office beyond that of Justice of the Peace. Her latter years were increasingly affected by bad health and she died on 19 September 1580, being buried at Spilsby church near her home. Richard died in 1582.[28]

Peregrine, of course had no claim to the throne, and neither did Henry or Charles, his half-brothers, because their parents transmitted none, but it was otherwise with the children of the French Queen. The Earl of Lincoln having died in 1534, that meant Frances and Eleanor, and the former of these was included in the extraordinary provision for the succession which Henry made by Act of Parliament in 1544. This statute (35 Henry VIII, cap. 1) declared Edward to be his father's heir, but then went on to say that in default of the birth of further sons to either of them, the Crown should pass to his natural daughters, Mary and Elizabeth, in that order, the only condition being that neither of them should marry without the consent of the Council.[29] They were not legitimated, and this was quite without precedent, because the common law had always forbidden the inheritance of bastards, and it was questionable whether statute could override the law in such a fashion.[30] Should all of his children die without progeny, the throne was to go to the children of his sister Mary, which meant Frances because Eleanor had died in 1539. This was remarkable in that it ignored the children of his elder sister, Margaret. These in 1544 consisted of her granddaughter by James V, Mary, who was already Queen of Scotland in her own right, and her daughter by her second marriage, Margaret Douglas, by then married to the Earl of Lennox. These children were unquestionably legitimate, and the only reason for their exclusion could have been that they were 'alien born', that is born outside the realm of England, but if that was the reason, then that was equally unprecedented. It seems more likely that the real reason for ignoring them was Henry's instinctive dislike of the Scots; however, none of this was specified in the Act. What was specified was that the arrangements so made could be altered or confirmed by the King's last will and testament, thus placing them firmly with the field of the royal prerogative, and opening the way for his son to do the like.[31] For the time being this was simply accepted, and Frances can have had little expectation of it becoming controversial.

Henry begot no more children after 1544, and in the summer of 1553 Edward was dangerously ill, a minor and still unmarried. However, he had a will of his own, and was determined not to be bound by his father's settlement. Above all he was determined to prevent any female from succeeding to the Crown. Before his illness became serious he had addressed the hypothetical question of what would happen if he were to die childless, and come up with a school exercise known as his 'Device'.[32] By the terms of this both Mary and Elizabeth were excluded as illegitimate, and Frances simply for being female. The Crown was to pass to any son whom she might bear, and failing that to the son of any daughter of hers. This was thinking long-term, because Frances had lost her only son as an infant and had not conceived for a number of years. Her eldest daughter, Jane, was fifteen and unmarried, while Catherine and Mary were younger still. As Edward's health deteriorated, the Device was simply not real politics, providing as it did for a regency in the event of no eligible male having been born. Something had got to be done, and either Edward or the Duke of Northumberland, who was his mentor at that stage, came up with the idea of including Jane Grey herself in the order of succession.[33] This could be done simply by amending the wording to read 'the lady Jane and her heirs male' as opposed to 'the heirs male of the Lady Jane'. It meant overcoming the King's prejudice against female rulers, but that was done. He liked Jane, and approved of her godliness, so if a woman had got to succeed, better her than the notoriously conservative Mary. The device was passed to the law officers as the King's will, to be translated into Letters Patent.[34] There were a number of problems with this. In the first place Frances had not resigned her right to her daughter, and should undoubtedly have taken precedence, and in the second place it was not clear that Edward, as a minor, could even make a valid will. Above all, there was Henry's unrepealed Act of Parliament making a totally different dispensation. Frances, however, did not press her claim, and it seems that nobody could stand the idea of the Duke of Suffolk as King Consort, so that when Edward died on 6 July, Jane was duly proclaimed. She was by then safely married to Guildford Dudley, the Duke of Northumberland's fifth son, so no question of consent arose and the Protestant succession seemed to be guaranteed for the foreseeable future. Or it would have been, had it not been for Mary, who rallied the aristocracy to her lawful cause, and overturned Jane's government in a matter of days.[35] The unfortunate Jane was consigned to the Tower, and executed the following February following Sir Thomas Wyatt's rising which was deemed to be aimed at replacing her on the throne. Her father, the Duke of Suffolk, who was most unwisely involved in the rebellion, was executed at the same time, and his lands forfeited to the Crown.[36] His widow, Frances, retreated to her dower lands and played no further part in public life before her own death in 1559.

Meanwhile the King's last succession Act continued in force, and when Mary's marriage to Philip of Spain failed to produce any offspring, Elizabeth became the heir, much to Mary's disgust.[37] It was, however, by popular acclaim that Henry's younger daughter succeeded her sister in November 1558, and that inevitably raised the Suffolk claim to the succession again. If the succession Act were ignored, then the next in line was Mary, Queen of Scots, a Catholic and married to the Dauphin of France; but in that event some would argue that she had a better claim than Elizabeth herself, since her legitimacy had never been questioned. This meant that the 1544 Act remained very much alive, and as the Queen evaded pressure to marry, Catherine Grey's claim was widely canvassed.[38] Most extraordinarily she became an object of interest to Philip II of Spain, who believed her to be a good Catholic, and who was desperate to prevent Mary of Scotland from succeeding to England and thus creating an Anglo-Scottish bloc under French protection. At the very beginning of Elizabeth's reign there were plots and rumours of plots, involving Catherine's abduction from England and marriage to a Habsburg prince – perhaps Don Carlos.[39] These rumours began to die away after the death of Francis II returned Mary to Scotland in August 1561, and in any case Catherine herself pre-empted them by a clandestine marriage in November of December 1560 to Edward Seymour, Earl of Hertford, the twenty-year-old son of Protector Somerset, a marriage which incidentally confirmed her Protestant credentials for the next round of the succession dispute. In 1561 she became pregnant and the secret of her wedding was revealed. Elizabeth was furious because one so close to the royal family should have obtained the Queen's consent to such a union, which manifestly she had not done. Elizabeth had no time for Catherine anyway, and committed her to the Tower, where she was joined a few weeks later by her unfortunate husband, who seems to have been an innocent party to the deception.[40] Edward, Lord Beauchamp, was born in the Tower in 1562, and an inquiry instituted into the lawfulness of the marriage. Given the Queen's attitude this inevitably found against the couple, and Catherine remained in confinement until she was released into house arrest in 1563. This dampened the enthusiasm of some of her supporters, but by no means all and her claim to the succession continued to be advanced in Protestant quarters down to her death in 1568, particularly in the parliament of 1566.[41]

Thereafter the Suffolk claim faded in to the background. Lord Beauchamp was considered to be illegitimate, and was in any case outlived by his father, while Thomas, who had been born after his mother emerged from the Tower, was both a younger son and a bastard. Mary, Catherine's sister, lived until 1578 but never inherited her sister's pretensions. She married humbly, again without the Queen's consent, and spent some time in prison as a result, but she was deformed and no one took her seriously as a claimant to the throne.[42] Eleanor's daughter, Margaret, was married suitably to Henry Stanley, the fourth Earl of Derby, and presumably obtained Elizabeth's consent to that union because she was not punished for failing to do so. Neither she nor her son ever put forward any claim, and no one did so on their behalf. Apart from some notional speculations in the 1590s, when the issue was very much alive owing to the Queen's failure to marry, the Suffolk line effectively died with Catherine. This left an embarrassing situation, because Henry's Act had simply specified that the Crown was to pass to the next lawful heir in the event that the Suffolk line failed. The most conspicuous claimant was Mary, Queen of Scots, whom Elizabeth persistently refused to exclude until she was eventually executed for conspiring against the Queen's life in 1587.[43] However, it was clear long before that that Mary was unacceptable to the Protestant elite, and after Catherine's death various alternatives were canvassed. The Howards had a claim, going back through the female line to Thomas of Woodstock, the sixth son of Edward III, and the Earl of Huntingdon a rather less remote one derived from his grandmother, Margaret, Countess of Salisbury, the daughter of George, Duke of Clarence (Edward IV's brother). Margaret Tudor's second marriage to the Earl of Angus was represented at this stage by Arabella Stuart, the granddaughter of Margaret Douglas, and the most remote claim of all was that proposed on behalf of the Infanta of Spain by Robert Parsons, which derived from a marriage by John of Gaunt, Edward III's fourth son, in the fourteenth century.[44] Of these the Infanta, the Earl of Huntingdon and Arabella Stuart were seriously supported by different interest groups, but the front-running contender was Mary's son, James VI of Scotland, whose father was Henry, Lord Darnley, Arabella's uncle, who had died in 1567.[45] James had been brought up as a Protestant, and thereby avoided his mother's fatal weakness, was unquestionably legitimate, and was an adult of proven competence. Elizabeth had made it clear that she did not consider his mother's fate a bar to his claim, and although she would not explicitly recognise him, by 1600 he was in touch with Robert Cecil, the Queen's powerful secretary, who had undertaken to smooth his passage.[46] So when Elizabeth died in 1603, James succeeded peacefully, and the long-running Tudor succession drama had finally come to an end. The 1544 Act was never repealed, because that would have raised questions about Elizabeth's own right to the throne, but it was quietly forgotten about. By the time that Edward Seymour's son, William, succeeded his grandfather as Earl of Hertford in 1621, it was no longer an issue and Mary Tudor's ghost was at last laid to rest.

APPENDIX 1
VERSES GREETING MARY ON HER ENTRY INTO PARIS

A ship represented Mary crossing the Channel, guided on its true course by the City of Paris. The sailors in the rigging sang her praises.

> Noble Lady, welcome to France,
> Through you we now shall live in joy and pleasure,
> Frenchmen and Englishmen live at their ease,
> Praise to God, who sends us such a blessing!

To which an orator responded:

> Most illustrious, magnanimous princess,
> Paris reveres and honours you
> And presents this ship to your nobility,
> Which is under the King's governance.
> Grains, wines and sweet liqueurs are therein,
> Which the winds propel by divine ordinance.
> All men of good will
> Receive you as Queen of France.

In the last tableau before the Palais Royale, the angel Gabriel presided over the Garden of France, where shepherds sang.

> As the peace between God and man,
> By the intervention of the Virgin Mary,
> Once was made, so now we,
> The French bourgeois are relieved of our burdens;
> Because Mary has married with us.
> Through her justice and peace join
> In the fields of France and in the countryside of England;
> Since the bonds of love hold in restraining arms,
> We have acquired for ourselves equally,
> Mary in heaven and Mary on earth.

(Taken from Charles Read Baskervill (ed.) *Pierre Grigore's Pageants for the Entry of Mary Tudor into Paris,* 1934. From BL Cotton MS Vespasian B.ii.)

APPENDIX 2
A SUFFOLK GARLAND

Eighth Henry ruling this land,

He had a sister fair,

That was the widowed Queen of France,

Enrich'd with virtues rare;

And being come to England's Court,

She oft beheld a knight,

Charles Brandon nam'd in whose fair eyes,

She chiefly took delight

And noting in her princely mind,

His gallant sweet behaviour,

She daily drew him by degrees,

Still more and more in favour;

Which he perceiving, courteous knight,

Found fitting time and place,

And thus in amorous sort began,

His love-suit to her grace.

....

Brandon (quoth she) I greater am,

Than would I were for thee,

But I can as little master love,

As them of low degree.

My father was a king, and so

A king my husband was,

My brother is the like, and he

Will say I do transgress.

But let him say what pleaseth him,

His liking I'll forego,

And chuse a love to please myself,

Though all the world said no:

If ploughmen make their marriages,

As best contents their mind,

Why should not princes of estate

The like contentment find?

But tell me, Brandon, am I not

More forward than beseems?

Yet blame me not for love, I love

Where best my fancy deems.

And long may live (quoth he) to love,

Nor longer live may I

Then when I love your royal grace,

And then disgraced die.

But if I do deserve your love,

My mind desires dispatch,

For many are the eyes in court,

That on your beauty watch:
But am I not, sweet lady, now
More forward than behoves?
Yet for my heart, forgive my tongue
That speaketh for him that loves.

The queen and this brave gentleman
Together both did wed,
And after sought the king's goodwill,
And of their wishes sped:
For Brandon soon was made a Duke,
And graced so in court,
And who but he did flaunt it forth
Amongst the noblest sort.

And so from princely Brandon's line,
And Mary did proceed
The noble race of Suffolk's house,
As after did succeed:
And whose high blood the lady Jane,
Lord Guildford Dudley's wife,
Came by descent, who with her lord,
In London lost her life.

(From the *Suffolk Garland; or a Collection of Poems, Songs, Tales, Ballads, Sonnets, and Elegies, Legendary and Romantic, Historical and Descriptive, Relative to that County*, 1818. The reader will observe that the poet's chronology in somewhat adrift!)

NOTES

Introduction: Historiography & Background

1. The Suffolk Garland is printed by W. C. Richardson in *Mary Tudor: The White Queen* (1970), pp. xiv–xvi. Jean de Prechac, *La Princesse d'Angleterre, ou la Duchesse Reyne* (Paris 1677), translated into English 1678. Marguerite de Lussan, *Marie d'Angleterre. Reine-Duchesse* (Amsterdam, 1749). Russell M. Garnier, *The White Queen* (London, 1899).

2. J.J. Scarisbrick, *Henry VIII* (London, 1968). S. J. Gunn, *Charles Brandon, Duke of Suffolk, 1484–1545* (Oxford, 1988). See also D. Loades, *Henry VIII* (Stroud, 2011).

3. Green, *Lives of the Princesses*, Vol. V. Both drew heavily on *The Union of the Two Noble Families of Lancaster and York* (edited by Richard Grafton in 1548), in the 1809 edition by Henry Ellis.

4. Mary Croom Brown, *Mary Tudor, Queen of France* (London, 1911). On the theoretical possibility of Mary's pregnancy, and the attentions of Francis, see also R. J. Knecht, *Francis I* (Cambridge, 1982), pp. 11–13.

5. M. K. Jones and M. G. Underwood, *The King's Mother. Lady Margaret Beaufort, Countess of Richmond and Derby* (Cambridge, 1992)

6. Erin A. Sadlack, *The French Queen's Letters: Mary Tudor Brandon and the Politics of Marriage in Sixteenth-Century Europe* (London, 2011).

7. John's father (also John) had been born to Katherine Swynford while she was still John of Gaunt's mistress. Their subsequent marriage had legitimated him, and this was confirmed by the Pope, but he was barred from any claim to the throne by Henry IV in 1407. Margaret's claim to the Crown depended upon whether this ban was accepted or not. This was controversial at the time, and since.

8. Jones and Underwood, *The King's Mother*, p. 61.

9. S. B. Chrimes, *Henry VII* (1972), p. 18.

10. Charles Ross, *Richard III* (1981). Edward had been betrothed to one

Eleanor Butler before he had married Elizabeth, and this was alleged to have created a pre-contract, thus making all his children illegitimate. This was an old and discredited story, resurrected for the occasion.

11. *The King's Mother*, pp. 62–5.

12. Chrimes, *Henry VII*, pp. 22–3.

13. John Morton, Lionel Woodville and Peter Courtenay.

14. For the agreement, see T. Rymer, *Foedera, Conventions, etc.* (London, 1704–35), XII, p. 226. By some means unknown, John Morton got wind of this intention, and warned Henry in time. Chrimes, *Henry VII*, p. 29.

15. Anne of Beaujeu was effectively Regent for her brother Charles VIII, and was concerned to avoid a confrontation with England during the minority.

16. These rumours seem to have been prompted by the thought that he would want to prevent her marriage to Henry, but that aim had been achieved by his agreement with the Queen Dowager over a year earlier.

17. R. A. Griffiths, *Sir Rhys ap Thomas and His Family* (1993)

18. Ibid. Chrimes, *Henry VII*, p. 43. *Cambrian Register* (1796), p. 83.

19. R. A. Griffiths and R. S. Thomas, *The Making of the Tudor Dynasty* (1985) is particularly good on the Bosworth campaign.

20. *Materials for a History of the Reign of Henry VII*, ed. W. Campbell (Rolls Series, 1873), I, p. 6.

21. No fewer than twenty-nine of his councillors had served Edward or Richard in the same capacity. J. R. Lander, 'The Yorkist Council and Administration, 1461–1485', *English Historical Review*, 72, 1958, pp. 27–46.

22. Chrimes, *Henry VII*, Appendix D, pp. 330–1.

23. *Rotuli Parliamentorum* (Records Commission, 1767–1832), VI, pp. 268–70.

24. S. Anglo, *Spectacle, Pageantry and Early Tudor Policy* (Oxford, 1969), pp. 18–21.

25. Chrimes, Appendix D, p. 330.

26. Richard Rex, *The Tudors* (Stroud, 2002), p. 16.

27. *Materials for a History of the Reign of Henry VII*, II, pp. 148 et seq.

28. After James was killed at Flodden, she married Archibald Douglas, Earl of Angus, and engaged in a long struggle for the control of her son, James V. She divorced Angus in 1527 and married Henry Stuart. Her last years were spent peacefully at the Scottish Court.

29. Erin A. Sadlack, *The French Queen's Letters*, p. 4.

30. J. J. Scarisbrick, *Henry VIII*.

1. The Infant Princess

1. This psalter remains in Exeter College Library in Oxford. Mary C. Brown, *Mary Tudor, Queen of France* (1911). The date of Mary's birth is also indicated by the authorisation of a payment of 50s by Privy Seal bill to the child's nurse, Anne Shenan, at Michaelmas 1496, suggesting that she was engaged in the spring. *Camden Miscellany*, 9, 1895.

2. The main nursery seems to have been at Richmond until the fire of 1497, at which point it was moved to Eltham.

3. W. C. Richardson, *Mary Tudor: The White Queen* (1970), p. 12.

4. H. M. Colvin, *The History of the King's Works* (1963–82), IV, ii, pp. 222–34.

5. Richardson, *Mary Tudor*, pp. 14–15.

6. *Privy Purse Expenses of Elizabeth of York*, ed. N.H. Nicolas (1830).

7. Ibid.

8. Jones and Underwood, *The King's Mother* (1992), p. 67.

9. Ibid.

10. St. John's College Archive D.4.10, notes 216–50.

11. Chrimes, *Henry VII*, p. 67, n. 3.

12. A. F. Pollard, *The Reign of Henry VII from Contemporary Sources* (1913/67), III, p. 231.

13. Chrimes, *Henry VII*, p. 295.

14. Richardson, *Mary Tudor*, p. 23.

15. Ian Arthurson, *The Warbeck Conspiracy, 1491–1499* (1994), pp. 146–161.

16. Raimondo de Raimondi, Milanese envoy in England to the Duke, 17 November 1498. *Calendar of State Papers, Milan, 1385–1618*, I, p. 358.

17. *Cal. Ven*, I, p. 790. 'News from London', 1 April 1499.

18. Erasmus, *Opus Epistolarum*, ed. P. S. and H. M. Allen (12 vols, 1906–58), I, no. 1.

19. Such as 'Giles the Luter' or 'The Welsh harpist'. Richardson, *Mary Tudor*, p. 24.

20. Ibid., pp. 27–8.

21. De Puebla to Ferdinand and Isabella, 15 July 1488, *Calendar of State Papers, Spanish*, I, p. 5.

22. G. Reese, *Music in the Renaissance* (1954), pp. 769 et seq.

23. Richardson, *Mary Tudor*, p. 27.

24. *De Institutione Feminae Christianae* (1524), in *Opera Omnia*, IV, pp. 65–301.

25. Rychard Hyrde's translation of Vives, *A Very Frutefull and Pleasant Boke* (1540).

26. Garrett Mattingly, *Catherine of Aragon* (1942), pp. 141–2.

27. Richardson, *Mary Tudor*, p. 30.

28. Chrimes, *Henry VII*, p. 93.

29. R. L. Storey, *The Reign of Henry VII* (1968), p. 62.

30. Polydore Vergil, *Anglica Historia*, ed. D. Hay (Camden Society, n.s., 74, 1950), pp. 142–3.

2. The Princess of Castile

1 A. H. Thomas and I. D. Thornley, *The Great Chronicle of London* (1938), pp. 312–15. S. Anglo, *Spectacle, Pageantry and Early Tudor Policy* (1969), pp. 100–3.

2. Mattingly, *Catherine of Aragon*, p. 55.

3. There was from the start dispute within the College of Cardinals as to the propriety of this dispensation, which partly at least accounts for the delay. Chrimes, *Henry VII*, p. 286.

4. The text of the declaration made by Prince Henry to Bishop Fox is printed in G. Burnet, *History of the Reformation*, ed. N. Pocock (1865), vol. 4, in the Collection of Records, pp. 17–18.

5. The report of these envoys is printed in *Memorials of King Henry VII*, ed. J. Gairdner (1858), pp. 223–39.

6. *Memorials*, p. 278.

7. Richardson, *Mary Tudor*, p. 34.

8. Anne had been the heir of Duke Francis II, who had died in 1488. She had been married originally to Charles VIII, and after his death in 1498 transferred (after a diplomatic divorce on his part) to his successor Louis XII.

9. This was a betrothal; the actual marriage did not take place until May 1514. The purpose, however, was to preserve the personal union in the event of Louis having no son.

10. Chrimes, *Henry VII*, p. 289. A partial account of the visit, written by an unknown contemporary, is printed in *Memorials*, pp. 282–303.

11. According to one chronicle, Mary and Catherine both enjoyed 'great cheer' during this visit. Charles Wriothesley, *A Chronicle of England*, ed. W. D. Hamilton (Camden Society, n.s., vol. XI, 1875).

12. Richardson, *Mary Tudor*, p. 36.

13. Thomas Brady et al. *A Handbook of European History, 1400–1600* (1994), pp. 446–54.

14. Where he remained until he was executed as a precaution by Henry VIII before his French campaign of 1513. His brother Richard was serving in the French army, and this is thought to have sealed his fate. J. J. Scarisbrick, *Henry VIII* (1968), p. 32.

15. This may have been because he did not get around to it before his death in September. The treaty was subsequently confirmed verbally (but not formally ratified) by Margaret of Savoy.

16. *Memorials*, pp. 282–303.

17. *Cal. Ven., 1202–1509*, pp. 883, 886. Vincenzo Quirini to the Signory, 25 June, 23 July 1506.

18. *Cal. Span.*, I, p. 502.

19. Ibid., p. 437. De Puebla to Ferdinand.

20. Sadlack, *The French Queen's Letters*, p. 16.

21. Ibid., p. 444. It is not clear that this clause was ever honoured.

22. Richardson, *Mary Tudor*, p. 39.

23. A. F. Pollard, *The Reign of Henry VII from Contemporary Sources* (1913/67), III, p. 128.

24. Petrus Carmelianus, *The solempnities & triumphes doon & made at the spousells and mariage of the kynges daughter, the ladye Marye*, ed. James Gairdner (Camden Miscellany, 9, no. 53 (2), 1893), p. 10.

25. Richardson, *Mary Tudor*, pp. 42–3.

26. Carmellianus, loc. cit.

27. Pollard, *The Reign of Henry VII*, III, p. 128.

28. Richardson, *Mary Tudor*, pp, 43–4.

29. Ibid.

30. Carmellinus, *The solempnities*, p. 15.

31. The only evidence for Henry's dying wish is contained in a letter written by Henry VIII to Margaret of Savoy on 27 June. *Letters and Papers … of the reign of Henry VIII*, ed. J. S. Brewer et al. (1862–1910), I, no. 84.

32. On Fuensalida's incompetence, see Mattingly, *Catherine of Aragon*, pp. 79–95. See also Pollard, *The Reign of Henry VII*, I, p. 317.

33. Pollard, loc. cit.

34. John Leland, *De Rebus Brittanicus Collectanea* (1715), IV, pp. 303–9. Richardson, *Mary Tudor*, pp. 57–8.

35. Chrimes, *Henry VII*, pp. 311–13. *The Will of Henry VII*, ed. T. Astle (1775).

36. Mary C. Brown, *Mary Tudor, Queen of France* (1911), p. 73.

37. On Catherine's appearance at this time, see Mattingly, p. 97.

38. Gutierre Gomez de Fuensalida, *Correspondencia*, ed. El Duque de Alba (1907), p. 518.

39. Edward Hall, *Chronicle* (ed. 1806), p. 507.

40. D. Loades, *The Fighting Tudors* (2009), pp. 40–59.

41. *Cal. Ven.*, II, p. 11. *Letters and Papers*, I, no. 156.

42. Richardson, *Mary Tudor*, p. 63.

43. Ibid. The Duke was acting 'by the aid and comfort of the French King'. Pollard, *The Reign of Henry VII*, p. 143.

44. Scarisbrick, *Henry VIII*, p. 26.

45. *Letters and Papers*, I, no. 1182. *Cal. Span.*, II, p. 131.

46. The naval campaign had not fared much better. A fleet had gone to Brest, but the only result of the campaign had been the loss of the *Regent* in dramatic circumstances. Alfred Spont, *The French War of 1512–13* (1897), pp. 49–50.

47. Rymer, *Foedera*, XIII, p. 354. *Letters and Papers*, I, nos. 1750, 1884. Charles Cruickshank, *Henry VIII and the Invasion of France* (1990), p. 82.

48. *Letters and Papers*, I, no. 276. The idea seems to have come originally from Maximilian.

49. Richardson, *Mary Tudor*, p. 67.

50. *Letters and Papers*, I, no. 1777.

51. Ibid., no. 2366, Declaration of 15 October 1513.

52. Cruickshank, *Invasion of France*, p. 163.

53. Polydore Vergil, *Anglica Historia*, p. 221. Scarisbrick, *Henry VIII*, pp. 37–8.

54. *Letters and Papers*, I, no. 2682.

55. Ibid., no. 2849

56. Ibid., no. 3101. This document also includes an oath by Louis XII to

observe the peace between the realms.
57. Richardson, *Mary Tudor*, p. 75.

3. The Politics of Marriage

1. Richardson, *Mary Tudor*, p. 76.
2. R. J. Knecht, *Francis I* (1982), pp. 242–3.
3. *Cal. Span.*, II, p. 164.
4. Ibid., pp. 159, 170.
5. *Calendar of State Papers, Milan* , pp. 686, 708–9. *Letters and Papers*, I, no. 2997.
6. *Cal. Ven.*, II, nos. 635, 695. Scarisbrick, *Henry VIII*, p. 53.
7. Message from Paris, 7 April 1514. *Letters and Papers*, I, no. 2791.
8. Ibid., no. 2957.
9. Rymer, *Foedera*, XIII, p. 413 et seq. *Letters and Papers*, I, no. 3131.
10. This response was accompanied, apparently, by Charles plucking a young hawk alive, to the consternation of his councillors. Richardson, *Mary Tudor*, p. 79.
11. Marino Sanuto, *Diarii*, ed. R. Fulin, F. Stefani et al. (1879–1903, Vol. XIX).
12. *Letters and Papers*, I, no. 3134. Richardson, *Mary Tudor*, p. 81.
13. *Letters and Papers*, I, no. 3146. Ibid.
14. *Cal. Ven.*, II, no. 500. Henry sent it to the jewellers of 'the Row' to have it valued, which was probably Middle Row near Staple Inn. This is close to Hatton Garden, the centre of the present diamond market. M. Perry, *Sisters to the King*, p. 129.
15. Venetian notes, 28 August 1514. *Letters and Papers*, I, no. 3206.
16. Ibid., no. 3247.
17. Perry, *Sisters*, p. 130.
18. Richardson, *Mary Tudor*, p. 84.
19. Ibid., p. 85.
20. *Cal. Ven.*, II, no. 500.
21. Hall, *Chronicle*, p. 570.
22. Ibid. Perry, *Sisters*, p. 133.
23. Richardson, *Mary Tudor*, p. 90.
24. Ibid., p. 91.
25. *Cal. Ven.*, II, no. 207.
26. Louis seems to have conducted himself in a remarkably youthful fashion throughout this encounter, not even dismounting in order to embrace her. *Les Memoires de Martin et Guillaume Du Bellay* (1753), VII, p. 184.
27. Carriages in the later sense were not known in the sixteenth century. These wagons were un-sprung, and drawn by anything from two to six horses. When carrying people, as here, they were normally highly decorated.
28. Richardson, *Mary Tudor*, p. 94.

29. *Cal. Ven.*, II, no. 511.

30. Ibid.

31. Ibid. Perry, *Sisters*, p. 139. Richardson, *Mary Tudor*, p. 95. The alarm bells were not rung, for fear of disturbing the King.

32. *Cal. Ven,* II, no. 511.

33. Ibid. Perry, *Sisters*, p. 138.

34. Du Bellay, VII, p. 187.

35. None of the numerous accounts of these events make mention of any expression of opinion on Mary's part. Presumably actions spoke louder than words. Du Bellay, VII, p. 187.

36. Hall, *Chronicle*, p. 571. *Letters and Papers*, I, ii, no. 3580. S. J. Gunn, *Charles Brandon, Duke of Suffolk* (1988), pp. 32–5.

37. *Cal. Span.*, II, p. 192. *Letters and Papers*, I, nos. 3472, 3476.

38. Ibid., p. 201.

39. *Letters and Papers*, I, ii, no. 3387.

40. Richardson, *Mary Tudor*, p. 114.

41. Hall, *Chronicle*, p. 571.

42. Du Bellay, VI, p. 184

43. *Letters and Papers*, I, no. 3355. Sadlack, *The French Queen's Letters*, p. 15.

44. D. Loades, *The Boleyns* (2011), p. 67. The exact date when Anne joined Mary's household is not known.

45. Perry, *Sisters*, p. 147.

46. Pierre Gringore, 'De la reception en entrée de la illustrissime dame et princesse Marie d'Agleterre … dans le ville de Paris le 6 Novembre 1514'. BL Cotton MS Vespasian B.II.

47. Hall, *Chronicle*, p. 571.

48. BL Cotton Vespasion B.II, f. 10.

49. Richardson, *Mary Tudor*, p. 118.

4. Mary as Queen of France

1. Richardson, *Mary Tudor*, pp. 119–20.

2. Ibid., p. 118.

3. Not all the continental observers would have agreed with this reservation, but in English accounts it is always the King who takes precedence. Perry, *Sisters to the King*, p. 149.

4. Jean de Autun, *Chroniques de Louis XII*, ed. R.de Maulde La Claviere (1889–93).

5. Dorset to Wolsey, 18 November 1514, *Letters and Papers*, I, ii, no. 3449.

6. Hall, *Chronicle*, p. 572.

7. Ibid., p. 573.

8. S. J. Gunn, *Charles Brandon*, pp. 32–5.

9. *Letters and Papers*, I, ii, no. 3472.

10. Ibid., nos. 3430, 3472, 3485. II, i, 1.

11. Richardson, *Mary Tudor*, p. 121.

12. Ibid.

13. This observer was the future Cardinal Jerome Alexander, who was quite accustomed to such occasions.

14. Suffolk to Wolsey, 7 November 1514, *Letters and Papers*, I, ii, no. 3424

15. Knecht, *Francis I*, p. 12.

16. Richardson, *Mary Tudor*, p. 124.

17. Francis's attitude to Mary at this juncture is a matter of some controversy. He may, or may not, have made improper suggestions – it depends on which source you read!

18. Robert de la Marck Fleuranges, *Histoire des choses memorables en France*, printed in *Les Memoires de Martin et Guillaume du Bellay* (1753).

19. Louise de Savoie, Journal, in J-A. C. Buchon, *Choix de chroniques et memoires relatif a l'Histoire de France* (1778–80), IV, pp. 457–64.

20. Jane had been banned by Louis on the ground of bad moral character (she had been the mistress of the Duke de Longueville) in spite of the fact that she had been Mary's childhood companion. The Queen was most upset.

21. Hall, *Chronicle*, p. 586.

22. Perry, *Sisters to the King*, p. 151.

23. The French crown was not strictly hereditary, 'for the new king is not the heir of his predecessor, and does not succeed in the possession of his goods …' The King succeeded by blood in accordance with the Salic Law. If Mary had borne a posthumous son to Louis XII, Francis would not have been the heir. Du Moulin, quoted by R. Doucet, *Les institutions de la France au XVIe siècle* (2 vols, 1948), I, p. 81.

24. Knecht, *Francis I*, p. 13.

25. Doucet, *Institutions*, I, 104–9. A. Lebey, *Le connetable de Bourbon* (1904), pp. 31–43.

26. Perry, *Sisters to the King*.

27. *Letters and Papers*, II, i, no. 46. BL Cotton MS Vespasian F.XIII, f. 281.

28. *Letters and Papers*, II, i, no. 80. BL Cotton MS Caligula D.VI. f. 179.

29. For a discussion of these negotiations, see Gunn, *Charles Brandon*, pp. 36–7.

30. *Letters and Papers*, II, i, no. 124.

31. Perry, *Sisters to the King*, p. 155.

32. BL Cotton MS Caligula D.VI, ff. 246–7.

33. *Letters and Papers*, II, i, no. 367. BL Cotton MS Vespasian F.XIII, f. 80.

34. Sadlack, *The French Queen's Letters*, pp. 101–10.

35. Richardson, *Mary Tudor*, p. 167.

5. Mary & the Duke of Suffolk

1. Polydore Vergil, *Anglica Historia*, ed. Hay, pp. 222–4.

2. Ibid.

3. Leo Had succeeded the warlike Julius II in March 1513.

4. Sadlack, *The French Queen's Letters*, p. 99.

5. Richardson, *Mary Tudor*, pp. 109–10.

6. Sadlack, p. 91.

7. Richardson, *Mary Tudor*, p. 132.

8. Sadlack, p. 98, which includes an exhaustive discussion of these drafts. Perry, *Sisters to the King*, p. 153.

9. *Letters and Papers*, II, i, nos. 85, 113.

10. Ibid., II, i. no. 227. TNA SP1/10, f. 79.

11. Vergil, *Anglica Historia*, pp. 228–9.

12. *Letters and Papers*, II, i, no. 80. BL Cotton MS Caligula D.VI, f. 186.

13. Perry, *Sisters to the King*, p. 153.

14. Sadlack, p. 178.

15. *Letters and Papers*, II, i, no. 222. BL Cotton MS Caligula D.VI, f. 176.

16. *Letters and Papers*, II, i, no. 203. Richardson, p. 180.

17. Perry, *Sisters to the King*, p. 154.

18. *Letters and Papers*, II, i, no. 223.

19. Sadlack, p. 178.

20. Ibid., pp. 180–1.

21. *Letters and Papers*, II, i, no. 436. Perry, *Sisters to the King*, p. 159.

22. Du Bellay, *Memoires*, VI, p. 185.

23. *Cal. Ven.* II, p. 618. This was in the process of admitting her own fault.

24. Gunn, *Charles Brandon*, p. 38.

25. *Letters and Papers*, II, i, nos. 224, 436. TNA, C54, 383.

26. Sadlack, p. 121.

27. Gunn, *Charles Brandon*, p. 2.

28. *Calendar of Inquisitions Post Mortem, 1485–95*, pp. 337–9.

29. *Materials for a History of the Reign of Henry VII*, ed. W. Campbell (1873–77), II, p. 495. Gunn, *Charles Brandon*, pp. 2–3.

30. TNA C24/28, 29. His aunt, Mary Redyng, was a gentlewoman to the Prince.

31. Gunn, *Charles Brandon*, pp. 6–7.

32. A. Spont, *The French Wars of 1512–13* (1897), pp. 145–53. Edward Echyngham to Wolsey, 5 May 1513.

33. Ibid., p. 147.

34. J. Anstis, *The Register of the Most Noble Order of the Garter* (1724), i, p. 275.

35. Hall, *Chronicle*, pp. 533, 566, 568.

36. Gunn, *Charles Brandon*, p. 9.

37. *Letters and Papers*, I, i, no. 698; ii, App. No. 9. Hall, *Chronicle*, pp. 510–12, 516, 518.

38. Ibid., p. 566, *Letters and Papers*, I, ii, no. 2575.

39. Hall, *Chronicle*, p. 526. Gunn, *Charles Brandon*, pp. 11–12.

40. *A Collection of Ordinances and Regulations for the Government of the Royal Household* (1790), p. 206. The personnel of the stables numbered 137 during Brandon's tour of duty, and its turnover was about £1,500 a year.

41. *Letters and Papers*, I, ii, nos. 1965, 1971, 1976, 1978, 1992.

42. The Guienne campaign had been a disaster because of the breakdown of discipline, something for which all the captains shared the responsibility. *Letters and Papers*, I, ii, no. 2575.

43. Gunn, *Charles Brandon*, p. 17

44. C. G. Cruikshank, *The English Occupation of Tournai, 1513–1519* (1971), pp. 7–8.

45. BL Harley Charter 43E8. *Descriptive Catalogue of Ancient Deeds in the Public Records Office*, V, A13349.

46. Helen Miller, *Henry the Eighth and the English Nobility* (1986).

47. Gunn, *Charles Brandon*, p. 33.

48. *Cal. Pat., 1494–1509*, p. 533. *Calendar of the Close Rolls, 1500–1509*, p. 316.

49. *Letters and Papers*, I, ii, nos. 2654, 2941.

50. *The Chronicle of Calais*, ed. J. G. Nichols (Camden Society 35, 1846), pp. 71–4. Hall, *Chronicle*, p. 566.

51. Elizabeth Grey was daughter and heir to Sir John Grey, Viscount Lisle; she was therefore Baroness Lisle in her own right when Brandon entered into his dubious contract with her, and he was granted the title on that consideration.

52. Sadlack, *Letters*, p. 182.

53. Richardson, *Mary Tudor*, pp. 183–5.

54. Gunn, *Charles Brandon*, pp. 42–3.

55. Ibid., pp. 39–40.

56. By 1516 he had been granted or had purchased 41 per cent of the total De la Pole holdings.

57. In East Anglia a queen attracted far more attention than a duke, and she received many presents and tributes. However the real test came at court, where their liveries were fully restored by 1519, and probably a good deal earlier. *Letters and Papers*, III. i, no. 491.

6. Mary, Suffolk & the King

1. *Cal. Ven.*, III, no. 88. *Rutland Papers*, ed. William Jerden (Camden Society, 21, 1842), pp. 28–49. Later, in January 1526 it was laid down that the Duke should always be lodged on the 'king's side' if the Duchess was not present. If they were both at court, they were to be lodged on the 'Queen's side'. *Letters and Papers*, III, no. 1939.

2. *Statutes of the Realm*, IV, I, p. 194. Approved on 20 December 1515. *Lords Journals*, Vol. I, p. 56.

3. Gunn, *Charles Brandon*, pp. 61–2.

4. *Letters and Papers*, II, ii, no. 4567.

5. Ibid., I, nos. 180, 197. J. de Iongh, *Margaret of Austria* (1954), p. 167.

6. *Letters and Papers*, II, ii, nos. 4061, 4134.

7. Ibid., II, I, nos. 834, 913, 1025, 1026, 1030. Gunn, *Brandon*, pp. 57–8.

8. *Letters and Papers*, Addendum I, no. 171. TNA SP1/232, ff. 6–8.

9. Gunn, *Brandon*, p. 61.

10. S. T. Bindoff, *The House of Commons, 1509–1558* (1982), II, p. 482. TNA IND 10217/1, f. 2.

11. *Letters and Papers*, II, i, no. 2170.

12. Gunn, *Brandon*, p. 58

13. *Letters and Papers*, II, ii, nos. 4061, 4134. Addendum, I, no. 210.

14. Ibid., II, ii, nos. 4303, 4346. TNA SP1/232, f. 81.

15. BL Cotton MS Vespasian D.I, f. 63. *Letters and Papers*, II, ii, Appendix, no. 48.

16. Ibid., no. 4448. TNA SP1/17, f. 67. Gunn, *Brandon*, p. 59.

17. *Letters and Papers*, III, i, nos. 14, 15.

18. Ibid., II, ii, no. 3872.

19. BL Harley Charter 43B1. BL Cotton MS Galba B.VI, f. 211. *Letters and Papers*, III, i, no. 926. Gunn, *Brandon*, p. 62.

20. Bod. MS Wood F.33, f. 45. TNA E179/69/4, 5. *Chronicle of Calais*, pp. 76–7. BL Egerton MS 985, ff. 61–4.

21. Gunn, *Brandon*, p. 63.

22. Ibid., p. 65.

23. Bod. MS Top. Berks . b.2, f. 13. TNA LR12/21/636.

24. *Letters and Papers*, II, i, no. 2170.

25. Ibid., no. 1935. E. Lodge, *Illustrations of British History* (1791), I, p. 17.

26. *Cal. Ven.*, II, p. 818. T. Malory, *The Works of Sir Thomas Malory*, ed. E. Vinaver (1947), II, pp. 568–70.

27. T. Rymer, *Foedera*, XIII, p. 624 et seq.

28. *Cal. Ven.*, III, p. 16.

29. For a full account of Wolsey's involvement in these arrangements, see J. G. Russell. *The Field of Cloth of Gold* (1969), pp. 16–21.

30. *Cal. Ven*, III, no. 61. Surian to the Doge and Senate, 3 June 1520. Scarisbrick, *Henry VIII*, pp. 77–8.

31. *Rutland Papers*, pp. 28–49.

32. Russell, *Field of Cloth of Gold*, pp. 95–104.

33. Ibid., p. 120.

34. *Cal. Ven.*, III, nos. 80, 84, 85.

35. Some thought that Anne Browne, the sister of Sir Wistan, outshone her, but this was not the general opinion. *Cal. Ven.*, III, nos. 50, 69.

36. Ibid., no. 78.

37. Russell, *Field of the Cloth of Gold*, pp. 160–4.

38. Ibid., p. 167.

39. *Cal. Ven.*, III, nos. 50, 90. A 'Chapel of Peace' was supposed to be erected on the site where the mass was held.

40. Scarisbrick, *Henry VIII*, p. 80. D. Loades, *Mary Tudor* (1989), p. 16.

41. Perry, *Sisters to the King*, p. 212.

42. Knecht, *Francis I*, pp. 105–6. England, which occupied the fourth side, thus assumed a disproportionate strategic importance.

43. Richardson, *Mary Tudor*, p. 277. *Letters and Papers*, V, pp. 750, 758.

44. Greg Walker, 'The Expulsion of the Minions in 1519 Reconsidered', *Historical Journal*, 32, 1989.
45. Perry, *Sisters to the King*, p. 212.
46. *Cal. Span.*, Further Supplement, pp. 195 et seq.
47. S. J. Gunn, 'The Duke of Suffolk's March on Paris in 1523', *English Historical Review*, 101, 1986.
48. *Letters and Papers*, IV, i, no. 61. Gunn, *Charles Brandon*, p. 76.
49. Gunn, 'The Duke of Suffolk's March'.
50. Gunn, *Charles Brandon*, p. 76.
51. *Letters and Papers*, IV, i, nos. 680, 841.
52. *Cal. Span.*, Further Supplement, pp. 388–9. Gunn, *Charles Brandon*, p. 77.
53. *Cal. Span.*, III, p. 315; Further Supplement, pp. 304, 348.
54. Ibid., III, p. 82.
55. G. W. Bernard, *War, Taxation and Rebellion in Early Tudor England: Henry VIII, Wolsey and the Amicable Grant of 1525* (1986), pp. 110–30.
56. Scarisbrick, *Henry VIII*, pp. 140–1.
57. *Cal. Ven.*, III, no. 1141.

7. The Duchess & Her Children

1. Richardson, *Mary Tudor*, p. 199.
2. Mattingly, *Catherine of Aragon*, pp. 131–2.
3. Richardson, p. 200. She was the widow of William Courtenay, who had been created Earl of Devon in May 1511, but had died a month later.
4. Although no one says so! Richardson, loc. cit.
5. Perry, *Sisters to the King*, p. 186.
6. Richard Grafton, *A Chronicle at Large* (ed. 1809), p. 288.
7. *Letters and Papers*, II, i, nos. 834, 913, 1025, 1026, 1030.
8. Gunn, *Charles Brandon*, p. 58.
9. Sadlack, *Letters*, p. 184. BL Cotton MS Caligila B.VI, f. 119
10. Richardson, p. 203.
11. *Letters and Papers*, II, ii, no. 3018. TNA SP1/15, f. 33.
12. Richardson, p. 205.
13. Grafton, *Chronicle*, p. 293.
14. Ibid., p. 294. Grafton gives no figures, but this is a rough estimate.
15. *Letters and Papers*, II, ii, no. 3712. BL MA Cotton Caligula B.I, f. 244. Grafton noted that all her expenses in England had been 'of the kings purse'.
16. *Cal. Ven*, II, pp. 918, 920. *Letters and Papers*, II, no. 1510.
17. *ODNB*. Richardson, *Mary Tudor*, pp. 210–11.
18. Hatfield was close to St Albans, and the Abbot no doubt well known to Nicholas West.
19. Gunn, *Charles Brandon*, p. 78. J. G. Nichols, 'Inventory of the Wardrobe, plate etc., of Henry Fitzroy, Duke of Richmond and Somerset', *Camden*

Miscellany, 3, 1855, pp. lxxxiv–v.

20. Walter Richardson ignored this child completely. *Mary Tudor*, p. 311.

21. Beyond the name of his tutor, nothing is known about Henry Brandon's schooling, nor whether it was any memory of her childhood that prompted Frances later to induce her husband to provide a first-rate education for their daughters.

22. *Letters and Papers*, III, ii, nos. 2927, 2944, 2960, 3276. TNA C54/398, m. 14.

23. TNA C54/392, m. 26 *Letters and Papers*, IV, ii, no. 4350. *Addendum*, I, no. 653.

24. Gunn, *Charles Brandon*, p. 131.

25. *Letters and Papers*, IV, ii, nos. 4246, 4257; IV, iii, no. 5859.

26. Gunn, *Charles Brandon*, p. 95.

27. *ODNB*.

28. A. G. Dickens, *The Clifford Letters of the Sixteenth Century* (Surtees Society, 1962), p. 24.

29. TNA WARDS9/149, f. 7. *Letters and Papers*, IV, iii, no. 5336 (12).

30. Gunn, *Charles Brandon*, p. 96.

31. Hall, *Chronicle*, p. 674.

32. *Cal. Ven*. IV, i, no. 965. Hall, p. 719.

33. Gunn, *Charles Brandon*, pp. 98–100

34. Ibid., p. 98.

35. *Letters and Papers*, IV, ii, nos. 2980, 4615, 4616. Knecht, *Francis I*, p. 186.

36. Ibid., IV, i, no. 2256; IV, ii, nos. 4392, 4615, 5064.

37. Gunn, *Charles Brandon*, p. 92.

38. R. Flenley, *Six Town Chronicles of England* (1911), p. 195. *Historical Manuscripts Commission: The Manuscripts of the Corporations of Southampton and Kings Lynn* (1887). p. 173.

39. BL Cotton MS Titus B.I, f. 71. *Letters and Papers*, II, i, no. 1605.

40. Gunn, *Charles Brandon*, pp. 78–82.

41. Norfolk Record Office, Register 14, ff. 135, 186, 210, 212. Translated by S. J. Gunn.

42. Richardson, *Mary Tudor*, pp. 213–4.

43. Ibid., p. 215. For the size of Wolsey's household, see P. J. Gwyn, *The King's Cardinal* (1990).

44. Gunn, *Charles Brandon*, pp. 78–83. For the Duke of Buckingham see Carole Rawcliffe, *The Staffords Earls of Stafford and Dukes of Buckingham* (1978), pp. 232–43.

45. Richardson, *Mary Tudor*, pp. 217–18.

46. Ibid.

47. Henry was annoyed with Suffolk on one occasion when he warned him not to pass through Woodstock, because one of the Duke's servants had died of the plague there. His annoyance was caused, however, by the thought that Suffolk should have warned him sooner. *Letters and Papers*, IV, ii, no. 2047.

48. Richardson, *Mary Tudor*, p. 119.

49. Ibid.

50. Brandon refers on a number of occasions to this ailment, without further elaboration, and the medical evidence of Mary's last illness is non-existent.

8. The Last Days

1. Perry, *Sisters to the King*, pp. 199–200.

2. *Letters and Papers*, IV, ii, no. 1939.

3. Richardson, *Mary Tudor*, pp. 213–14.

4. Gunn, *Charles Brandon*, p. 113.

5. J. A. Guy, *The Public Career of Sir Thomas More* (1980), p. 116.

6. Shilston died shortly after his election and his will was witnessed by ducal servants. TNA PROB11/24/3. Gunn, *Brandon*, p. 114.

7. *Letters and Papers* , IV, iii, nos. 6225, 6262, 6436, 6575, 6738.

8. Ibid., V, nos. 40, 45, 70, 564, 864, 932.

9. Ibid., VII, no. 296; VIII, no. 342.

10. Ibid., V, no. 287.

11. Mattingly, *Catherine of Aragon*, p. 271.

12. *Cal. Span.*, IV, ii, pp. 892–3, 895–9.

13. Carlo Capello to the Doge and Signory, 23 April 1532. *Cal. Ven.*, IV, no. 761.

14. Ibid., no. 802.

15. *Letters and Papers*, IV, i, no. 2744.

16. Ibid., V, no. 199. There are various calculations of these rates of payment, and the actual sum received appears to have depended upon what deductions were made for collection and other expenses.

17. Ibid., no. 361.

18. Ibid., VI, no. 293.

19. Gunn, *Charles Brandon*, p. 120. Suffolk seems to have got his own back by passing some derogatory comments on Cromwell to the French ambassador. *Letters and Papers*, VI, no. 1372.

20. E. W. Ives, *The Life and Death of Anne Boleyn* (2004), pp. 172–83. 'The Noble Triumphant Coronation of Queen Anne', in A. F. Pollard, *Tudor Tracts* (1903), pp. 9–28.

21. *Letters and Papers*, VII, no. 1498 (37). TNA SP1/75, f. 245.

22. Richardson, *Mary Tudor*, pp. 252–3.

23. *Letters and Papers*, VI, no. 693. BL Harley MS 6986, f. 11. Sadlack, *Letters*, p. 154.

24. Richardson, *Mary Tudor*, pp. 254–5.

25. *Chronica del rey Enrico de Inglaterra* (The Chronicle of King Henry VIII of England), translated by M. A. S. Hume (1889).

26. The Baillie of Troyes to Francis I, 30 June 1533. *Letters and Papers*, VI, no. 723.

27. Richardson, *Mary Tudor*, p. 257.

28. Royal College of Arms, Heralds' MSS. Francis Ford, *Mary Tudor: A Retrospective Sketch* (1882) pp. 38–45.

29. Richardson, *Mary Tudor*, p. 260.

30. Ibid., p. 261.

31. It is suggested that she may have helped him to the abbacy three years earlier. *ODNB*.

32. The abbey church was gutted at the dissolution.

33. As Edward Foxe reported to Lord Lisle. *Letters and Papers*, VI, no. 797.

34. When a similar celebration was suggested for his own ex-Queen, Catherine, the King observed 'that it should be more charge than was either requisite or necessary'.

35. The cost can only be guessed at, but in 1579 Sir Thomas Gresham's burial cost £800, and in 1588 the Earl of Leicester's nearly £3,000. Mary's obsequies probably cost the Duke about £1,000, over and above what was spent in London.

36. *Cal. Span.*, IV, ii, p. 1123. Felicity Heal, *Of Prelates and Princes* (1980), p. 108.

37. Gunn, *Charles Brandon*, pp. 132–3.

38. *Statutes of the Realm*, IV, i, p. 295. 27 Henry VIII, c. 39. Lincolnshire R.O. 2Anc3/B/5.

39. For a brief account of the property manipulations attendant upon changes in the incumbents of sees, see Heal, *Prelates and Princes*, pp. 134–5.

40. *Letters and Papers*, IX, no. 139.

41. *Catalogue des Actes de Francios Ier* (1887–1908), II, 6074, VII, 29115, 29203.

42. *Letters and Papers*, VI, no. 1434. *Catalogue des Actes*, II, 6426, 6604, 6618. Gunn, *Charles Brandon*, pp. 140–1.

43. *Cal. Span.*, V, i, p. 114.

44. M. St Clare Byrne, *The Lisle Letters* (1981), IV, p. 164, n. 1. *Letters and Papers*, IX, nos. 217, 386.

9. The Legacy

1. J. A. Guy, *The Public Career of Sir Thomas More*, p. 59. TNA STAC2/17/399; 19/241.

2. *The Clifford Letters of the Sixteenth Century*, ed. A. G. Dickens (Surtees Society, 1962), pp. 24, 141. 'The Clifford Letters', ed. R. W. Hoyle (*Camden Miscellany*, 44, 1992, pp. 102–14). *Statutes of the Realm*, IV, i, p. 587. 27 Henry VIII, c. 36.

3. M. H. and R. Dodds, *The Pilgrimage of Grace, 1536–1537, and the Exeter Conspiracy, 1538* (1915), I, pp. 119–20. Gunn, *Charles Brandon*, p. 144.

4. *Letters and Papers*, XI, nos. 600, 661, 680, 808.

5. Ibid., nos. 716, 756, 773, 808.

6. Gunn, *Charles Brandon*, p. 147.

7. *State Papers*, I, p. 522.

8. For the terms of the Pontefract agreement see R. W. Hoyle, *The Pilgrimage of Grace and the Politics of the 1530s* (2001), pp. 460–3.

9. *Letters and Papers*, XII, i, nos. 636, 1284.

10. Ibid., XV, no. 942 (52). Lincoln R.O. 2Anc 1/5.6, 3/A/ 48, 49.

11. Gunn, *Charles Brandon*, pp. 154–6.

12. *Letters and Papers*, XIV, ii, no. 342. Addendum, ii, no. 1414.

13. TNA C54/425. Lincolnshire R.O. 1Anc.11/C/1a.

14. *Lisle Letters*, IV, nos. 845a, 874–5, 880, 901.

15. D. Loades, *The Tudor Court* (1986), p. 204. Gunn, *Charles Brandon*, pp. 178–9.

16. C. Wriothesley, *A Chronicle of England*, ed. W. D. Hamilton (Camden Society, 1875), I, pp. 80, 96.

17. *State Papers*, V, p. 306.

18. *Letters and Papers*, XIX, ii, no. 483.

19. Ibid., nos. 5, 222, 236, 276, 424.

20. Gunn, *Charles Brandon*, p. 193.

21. *Letters and Papers*, XIX, ii, nos. 353, 365, 374, 377, 383, 395, 402, 415.

22. Only half of this purchase price was paid in cash. TNA E318/20/1079, mm. 3–5.

23. TNA SC12/23/29, ff. 4–5. Lincoln R.O. 2Anc3/A/49.

24. D. MacCulloch, *Suffolk and the Tudors* (1986), p. 159.

25. Susan Brigden, 'Popular Disturbance and the Fall of Thomas Cromwell and the Reformers, 1539–40', *Historical Journal*, 24, 1981, p. 266. J. Foxe, *Acts and Monuments* (ed. 1583), p. 1206.

26. Gunn, *Charles Brandon*, pp. 198–9.

27. C. Garrett, *The Marian Exiles* (1966), pp. 87–9. Foxe, *Acts and Monuments* pp. 2078-80.

28. *ODNB*.

29. *Statutes of the Realm*, IV, i. pp. 955–8.

30. E. W. Ives, 'Tudor Dynastic Problems re-visited', *Historical Research*, 81, 2008.

31. Ibid.

32. Inner Temple MS Petyt xlvii, f. 316. Printed and edited in J. G. Nichols (ed.) *The Literary Remains of King Edward VI* (Roxburgh Club, 1857), II, pp. 571–2.

33. D. Loades, *John Dudley, Duke of Northumberland* (1996), pp. 240–1. E. W. Ives, *Lady Jane Grey* (2009), pp. 151–4.

34. This was done, but the patent never passed the Seals, so it had no status in law. The force of the Device therefore depended entirely upon Edward's prerogative power. Ives, *Jane Grey*, pp. 166–8.

35. D. Loades, *Mary Tudor: A Life* (1989), pp. 171–82.

36. D. Loades, *Two Tudor Conspiracies* (1965), p. 115.

37. Mary had made it clear before her marriage that, in the event of her leaving no heir of her body, she did not wish Elizabeth to succeed.

Cal. Span., XI, p. 393.

38. For a full exploration of Catherine's claim and its supporters, see Mortimer Levine, *The Early Elizabethan Succession Question* (1966).

39. Ibid., pp. 14–15.

40. If the marriage had been conducted in the presence of witnesses (as this was), it would have constituted a binding contract *per verba de praesenti* until the law was changed in 1753. Ibid., p. 27.

41. Ibid., pp. 165–98.

42. Cecil to Sir Thomas Smith, 21 August 1565. Ellis, *Original Letters*, II, ii, p. 299.

43. W. MacCaffrey, *Queen Elizabeth and the Making of Policy, 1572–88* (1981), pp. 480–1.

44. Parsons (writing as 'R. Dolman'), *A Conference about the Next Succession to the Crowne of England* (1594).

45. G. R. Elton, *England under the Tudors* (1955), genealogical tables.

46. David Loades, *The Cecils* (2007), pp. 219-223.

BIBLIOGRAPHY

Manuscripts

British Library
Cotton MS
    Caligula B.1, B.VI, D.VI
    Galba B.VI
    Vespasian B.II, F.XIII
Egerton MS 985
Harley MS 6986
Harley Charter 43E8

The National Archives
C.24, 54
E179
PROB11
STAC2
SP1
WARDS9

The Lincoln Record Office citations are taken from S. J. Gunn, *Charles Brandon, Duke of Suffolk, 1484–1545* (Oxford, 1988).

Printed Sources

Primary Works
Anstis, J., *The Register of the Most Noble Order of the Garter* (1724).

Astle, J., *The Will of Henry VII* (1775).

Autun, Jean de, *Chronique de Louis XII*, ed. R. de Maulde La Claviere (1889–93).

Boleyn, Anne, 'The Most Noble Coronation of Queen Anne', in A. F. Pollard, *Tudor Tracts* (1903).

Du Bellay, *Les Memoires de Martin et Guillaume du Bellay* (1753).

Byrne, M. St Clare (ed.), *The Lisle Letters* (1981).

Calendar of the Close Rolls, 1500–1509 (1963).

Calendar of Inquisitions Post Mortem, 1485–95 (1898).

Calendar of the Patent Rolls, 1494–1509 (1916).

Calendar of State Papers, Milan, ed. A. B. Hinds (1912)

Calendar of State Papers, Spanish, ed. Royall Tyler et al. (1862–1954).

Calendar of State Papers, Venetian, ed. R. Brown et al. (1864–98).

Campbell, W. (ed.), *Materials for a History of the Reign of Henry VII* (Rolls Series, 1873).

Carmelianus, Petrus, *The solempnities & triumphes doon & made at the spousells and mariage of the kynges daughter, the ladye Marye*, ed. James Gairdner (Camden Miscellany, 9, no. 53 (2), 1893).

Catalogue des Actes de Francois Ier (1887–1908).

Chronica del Rey Enrico de Inglaterra (The Chronicle of King Henry of England) trans. M. A. S. Hume (1889).

A Collection of Ordinances and Regulations for the Government of the Royal Household (1790).

A Descriptive Catalogue of Ancient Deeds in the Public Records Office (1915).

Dickens, A. G. (ed.), *The Clifford Letters of the Sixteenth Century* (Surtees Society, 1962).

Erasmus, Desiderius, *Opus Epistolarum*, ed. P. S. and N. M. Allen (12 vols, 1906–58).

Flenly, R., *Six Town Chronicles of England* (1911).

Foxe, John, *The Actes and Monuments of the English Martyrs* (1583).

Fuensalida, *Correspondencia de Gutierre Gomez de Fuensalida*, ed. El Duque de Alba (1907).

Grafton, Richard, *A Chronicle at Large* (1809).

The Great Chronicle of London, ed. A. H. Thomas and I. D. Thornley (1938).

Hall, Edward, *Chronicle* (1806).

Historical Manuscripts Commission, *Manuscripts of the Corporations of Southampton and Kings Lynn* (1887).

Hoyle, R. W. (ed.), 'The Clifford Letters' (*Camden Miscellany*, 44, 1992).

Leland, John, *De Rebus Brittanicus Collectanea* (1715).

Letters and Papers, Foreign and Domestic, of the Reign of King Henry VIII, ed. J. S. Brewer et al. (1862–1932).

Louise de Savoie, *Journal*, in J-A. C. Buchon, *Choix de Choniques et Memoires relative a l'Histoire de France* (1778–80).

Malory, Sir Thomas, *The Works of Sir Thomas Malory* ed. E. Vinover (1947).

Memorials of King Henry VII, ed. J. Gairdner (1858).

Nicholas, N. H., *The Privy Purse Expenses of Elizabeth of York* (1830).

Nichols, J. G. (ed.), *The Chronicle of Calais* (Camden Society, 36, 1846).

Nichols, J. G. (ed.), 'Inventory of the Wardrobe, plate etc. of Henry Fitzroy,

Duke of Richmond and Somerset' (*Camden Miscellany*, 3, 1855).

Nichols, J. G., *The Literary Remains of King Edward VI* (Roxburgh Club, 1851).

Parsons, R. (R. Doleman), *A Conference about the Next Succession to the Crowne of England* (1594).

Pollard, A. F., *The Reign of Henry VII from Contemporary Sources* (1913, reprinted 1967)

Rotuli Parliamentorum (Records Commission, 1767–1832).

Rutland Papers, ed. W. Jerdan (Camden Society, 12, 1842).

Rymer, T., *Foedera, Conventions, etc.* (1704–35).

Sadlack, Erin, *The French Queen's Letters* (2011).

Sanuto, Mario, *Diarii*, ed. R. Futin, F. Stephen et al. (1879–1903).

Spont, Alfred, *The French Wars of 1512–13* (Navy Records Society, 1897).

Statutes of the Realm, ed. A. Luders et al. (1810–28).

Vergil, Polydore, *Anglica Historia*, ed. D. Hay (Camden Society, 3rd series, 4, 1950).

Wriothesley, Charles, *A Chronicle of England*, ed. W. D. Hamilton (Camden Society, 48, 1875).

Secondary Works

Anglo, S., *Spectacle, Pageantry and Early Tudor Policy* (1969).

Arthurson, Ian, *The Warbeck Conspiracy 1491–1499* (1994).

Bernard, G. W., *War, Taxation and Rebellion in Early Tudor England: Henry VIII, Wolsey and the Amicable Grant of 1525* (1986).

Bindoff, S. T., *The House of Commons, 1509–1558* (1982).

Brady, T., et al., *A Handbook of European History, 1400–1600* (1994).

Brigden, Susan, 'Popular Disturbances and the Fall of Thomas Cromwell and the Reformers, 1539–40', *Historical Journal*, 24, 1981.

Brown, Mary C., *Mary Tudor, Queen of France* (1911).

Burnet, Gilbert, *History of the Reformation*, ed. N. Pocock (1865).

Chrimes, S. B., *Henry VII* (1972).

Colvin, H. M., *A History of the King's Works* (1963–82).

Cruickshank, C. G., *Henry VIII and the Invasion of France* (1990).

Dodds, M. H. and R., *The Pilgrimage of Grace, 1536–7, and the Exeter Conspiracy, 1538* (1915).

Doucet, R., *Les institutions de la France au XVIe siècle* (1948).

Elton, G. R., *England under the Tudors* (1955).

Elton, G. R. *The Tudor Constitution* (1982).

Ford, Francis, *Mary Tudor: A Retrospective Sketch* (1882).

Garrett, Christina, *The Marian Exiles* (1966).

Garnier, Russell H., *The White Queen* (1899).

Griffiths, R. A., and R. S. Thomas, *The Making of the Tudor Dynasty* (1985).

Griffiths, R. A., *Sir Rhys ap Thomas and His Family* (1993).

Gunn, S. J., 'The Duke of Suffolk's March on Paris in 1523', *English Historical Review*, 101, 1986.

Gunn, S. J., *Charles Brandon, Duke of Suffolk, 1484–1545* (1988).

Guy, J. A., *The Public Career of Sir Thomas More* (1980).

Gwyn, P. J., *The King's Cardinal* (1990).

Heal, Felicity, *Of Prelates and Princes* (1980).

Hoyle, R. W., *The Pilgrimage of Grace and the Politics of the 1530s* (2001).

Jones, M. K., and M. G. Underwood, *The King's Mother: Lady Margaret Beaufort, Countess of Richmond and Derby* (1992).

Iongh, Jane de, *Margaret of Austria* (1954).

Ives, E. W., *The Life and Death of Anne Boleyn* (2004).

Ives, E. W., 'Tudor Dynastic Problems Revisited', *Historical Research*, 81, 2008.

Ives, E. W., *Lady Jane Grey: A Tudor Mystery* (2009).

Knecht, R. J., *Francis I* (1982).

Lander, J. R., 'The Yorkist Council and Administration 1461–1485', *English Historical Review*, 72, 1958.

Levine, Mortimer, *The Early Elizabethan Succession Question* (1966).

Loades, D., *Two Tudor Conspiracies* (1965).

Loades, D., *The Tudor Court* (1986).

Loades, D., *Mary Tudor: A Life* (1989).

Loades, D., *John Dudley, Duke of Northumberland* (1996).

Loades, D., *The Fighting Tudors* (2009).

Loades, D., *Henry VIII* (2011).

Loades, D., *The Boleyns* (2011).

Loades, D., *The Tudors* (2012).

Lodge, E., *Illustrations of British History* (1791).

MacCaffrey, W., *Queen Elizabeth and Making of Policy, 1572–1588* (1981).

MacCulloch, D., *Suffolk and the Tudors* (1986).

Mattingly, Garrett, *Catherine of Aragon* (1963).

Miller, Helen, *Henry VIII and the English Nobility* (1986).

Perry, Maria, *Sisters to the King* (1998).

Rawcliffe, Carole, *The Stafford Earls of Stafford and Dukes of Buckingham* (1978).

Reese, G., *Music in the Renaissance* (1954).

Rex, Richard, *The Tudors* (2002).

Richardson, W. C., *Mary Tudor: The White Queen* (1970).

Ross, Charles, *Richard III* (1981).

Russell, J. G., *The Field of Cloth of Gold* (1969).

Scarisbrick, J. J., *Henry VIII* (1968).

Storey, R. L, *The Reign of Henry VII* (1968).

Walker, Greg, 'The Expulsion of the Minions in 1519 Reconsidered', *Historical Journal*, 32, 1989.

LIST OF ILLUSTRATIONS

1. Author's collection.
2. From a private collection.
3. © Jonathan Reeve JR2516b11p7 15001550.
4. © Josphine Wilkinson.
5. © Elizabeth Norton.
6. © Elizabeth Norton, © Stephen Porter.
7. © Ripon Cathedral.
8. © Elizabeth Norton.
9. © Ripon Cathedral.
10. © Jonathan Reeve JR1151b66p1 15001550.
11. & 12. © Jonathan Reeve JR1872b46fp16 13001350. © Jonathan Reeve JR1884b46fp192 15001550.
13. © Jonathan Reeve JR1873b46fp22 15001550.
14. © Jonathan Reeve JR1874b46fp28 15001550.
15. © Jonathan Reeve JR1875b46fp34 15001550.
16. © Jonathan Reeve JRCD3b20p1025 15501600.
17. © Jonathan Reeve JR1169b2p7 15001550.

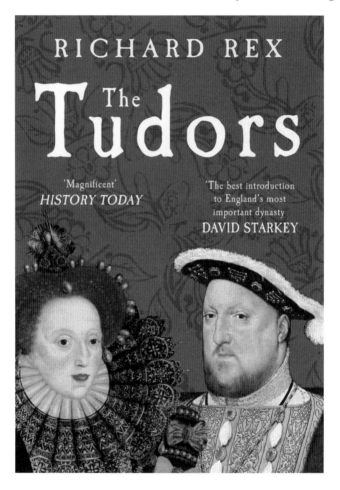

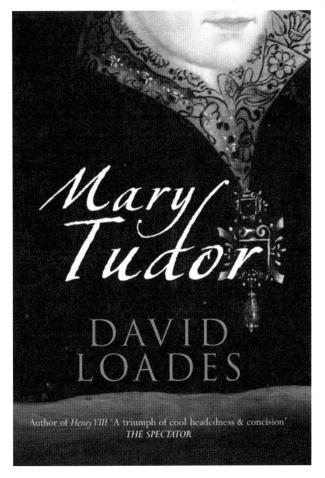

Also available from Amberley Publishing

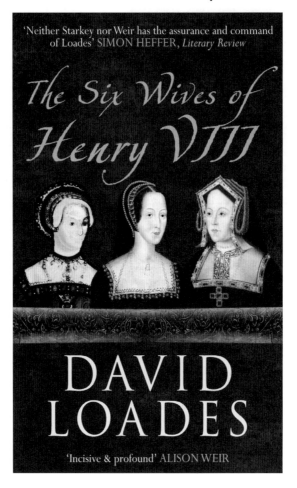

The marital ups and downs of England's most infamous king

'Neither Starkey nor Weir has the assurance and command of Loades'
SIMON HEFFER, LITERARY REVIEW

'Incisive and profound... I warmly recommend this book' ALISON WEIR

The story of Henry VIII and his six wives has passed from history into legend – taught in the cradle as a cautionary tale and remembered in adulthood as an object lesson in the dangers of marrying into royalty. The true story behind the legend, however, remains obscure to most people, whoe knowledge of the affair begins and ends with the aide memoire 'Divorced, executed, died, divorce, executed, survived'.

£9.99 Paperback
55 illustrations (31 colour)
224 pages
978-1-4456-004-9

Available from all good bookshops or to order direct
Please call **01453-847-800**
www.amberleybooks.com

Also available from Amberley Publishing

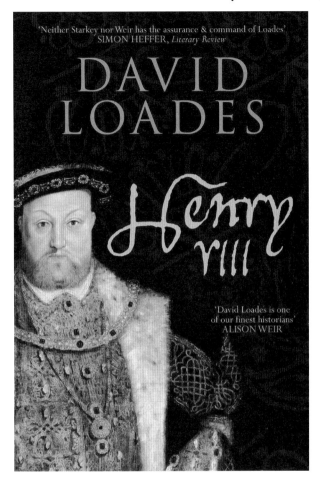

A major new biography of the most infamous king of England

'A triumph' THE SPECTATOR

'The best place to send anyone seriously wanting to get to grips with alternative understandings of England's most mesmerising monarch... copious illustrations, imaginatively chosen' BBC HISTORY MAGAZINE

'David Loades Tudor biographies are both highly enjoyable and instructive, the perfect combination' ANTONIA FRASER

Professor David Loades has spent most of his life investigating the remains, literary, archival and archaeological, of Henry VIII, and this monumental new biography book is the result. As a youth, he was a magnificent specimen of manhood, and in age a gargantuan wreck, but even in his prime he was never the 'ladies man' which legend, and his own imagination, created. Sexual insecurity undermined him, and gave his will that irascible edge which proved fatal to Anne Boleyn and Thomas Cromwell alike.

£25 Hardback
113 illustrations (49 colour)
512 pages
978-1-84868-532-1

Available from all good bookshops or to order direct
Please call **01453-847-800**
www.amberleybooks.com

Also available from Amberley Publishing

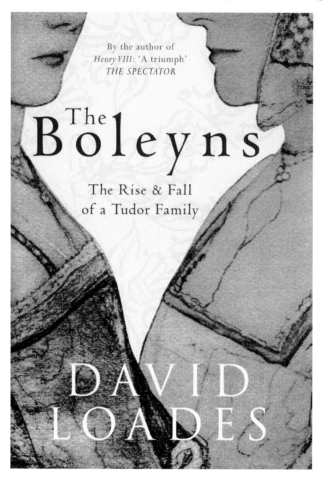

By the author of
Henry VIII: 'A triumph'
THE SPECTATOR

The Boleyns

The Rise & Fall of a Tudor Family

DAVID LOADES

A magnificent tale of family rivalry and intrigue set against Henry VIII's court

The fall of Anne Boleyn and her brother George is the classic drama of the Tudor era. The Boleyns had long been an influential English family. Sir Edward Boleyn had been Lord Mayor of London. His grandson, Sir Thomas had inherited wealth and position, and through the sexual adventures of his daughters, Mary and Anne, ascended to the peak of influence at court. The three Boleyn children formed a faction of their own, making many enemies: and when those enemies secured Henry VIII's ear, they brought down the entire family in blood and disgrace.

£20 Hardback
50 illustrations (25 colour)
352 pages
978-1-4456-0304-9

Available from all good bookshops or to order direct
Please call **01453-847-800**
www.amberleybooks.com

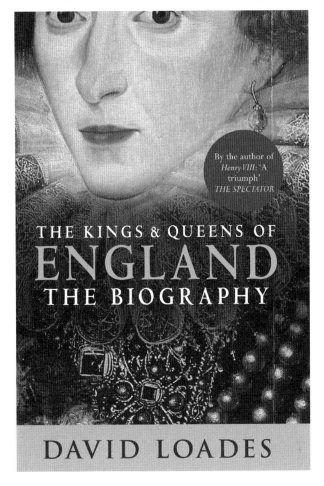

INDEX